PLANTS FOR PROFIT

INCOME OPPORTUNITIES IN HORTICULTURE

by
Francis X. Jozwik
Ph.D.—Plant Science

Andmar Press
West Yellowstone Avenue
P.O. Box 217
Mills, WY 82644-0217

Library of Congress Catalog
Card Number: 84-70515
ISBN: 0-916781-21-6

Printed in the United States of America

CIP

Jozwik, Francis X.
    Plants for profit; income opportunities in
horticulture/ by Francis X. Jozwik. -- 2nd ed.
    p. cm.
    Includes bibliographical references and index.
    LCCN: 84-70515
    ISBN: 0-916-781-21-6

    1. Greenhouse management. 2. Horticulture
3. New agricultural enterprises. I. Title

SB415.J69 2000   635.9'823
                            QB199-1197

CONTENTS

ABOUT THE AUTHOR

Francis Jozwik received a Ph.D. in Plant Science from the University of Wyoming in 1966. He began his professional career lecturing in plant physiology with the University of Wisconsin System and later was appointed to the position of Arid Lands Research Scientist in the Commonwealth Scientific and Industrial Research Organization of Australia.

In addition to his scientific and academic background, Dr. Jozwik has become active in commercial horticulture as the owner of a successful greenhouse and nursery business. The wide experience Dr. Jozwik has acquired both as a scientist and in private industry assure that his books and articles are technically correct while possessing a down-to-earth style.

Who's Who In America has honored Dr. Jozwik for his professional accomplishments by repeatedly including his biography in that publication. The National Science Foundation has supported some of his basic research in the field of biosystematics.

Readers of the present book who wish to investigate specific details of commercial ornamental plant culture more thoroughly will find a larger volume entitled *The Greenhouse and Nursery Handbook* useful for further study. Ordering information for that title and others by Dr. Jozwik is available near the back cover.

DISCLAIMER

This book is intended to present information about commercial activity within certain subject areas of horticulture. While the author and publisher have carefully attempted to make this information reliable and timely, readers should note that a good deal of it is based upon personal experiences and observations of the author. The validity of the information and viewpoints can differ with circumstances; therefore, neither the author nor publisher guarantees the accuracy of the text material under all situations.

No attempt has been made to make the present book a final and ultimate source of information about the subject matter involved. Readers should always study further sources in order to complement, amplify, and confirm the present text.

Beginning a business in specialized horticulture is not a get rich quick scheme. Although many people have become extremely successful in this field, most have accomplished the feat only after working hard and smart.

The author and Andmar Press shall have no liability or responsibility to any individual or entity experiencing loss or damage, or alleged loss or damage, thought to be caused directly or indirectly by information presented in this book.

Readers who have purchased this book directly from Andmar Press and who do not wish to accept the above conditions in full may feel free to return the book to the publisher for a refund of the purchase price. The original Andmar Press invoice along with the customer's name and address must accompany all refund requests.

If you purchased the book from any independent agent other than Andmar Press, you must follow their refund policies.

INTRODUCTION

During the many years I have worked as a university professor and commercial horticulturist, numerous people have asked me to counsel them about how to start their own career in this fulfilling and profitable industry.

Over time, this consulting work began to occupy a good deal of my interest and daily activity. In response to these additional duties, I decided to organize all the information people required into a coherent series of books which covered the material progressively from introductory principles through the highly technical data a person might need to operate a successful greenhouse or nursery.

The book you now have in hand is, for the most part, generalized and designed to give persons interested in a horticultural career a quick overview which can be easily understood, even if they lack an amateur background in gardening, landscaping or other aspects of plant culture. *Plants for Profit* will also expose beginners to a wide variety of opportunities in horticulture. The field studies in particular should broaden every reader's understanding of the numerous possibilities open to exploration as career choices.

While most people who seek advice are interested from an entrepreneurial standpoint, a significant number wish to begin their careers working for an established business or institution, thereby gaining valuable experience before striking out on their own. This is why I have included an extensive section about how to find jobs in horticulture. Working for someone else is often the most sensible thing to do as a beginner. You accumulate a lot of knowledge about the field and get paid a salary in the process. Not a bad deal!

In *Plants for Profit,* I want to first give readers a glimpse into how they might start their own commercial horticulture business. I will then present some general principles concerning how to grow and market plants. A later chapter about private label potting soil illustrates how related profit centers can make a good business even more successful. This chapter introduces you to the many details which must be taken care of when setting up a specific horticultural business. It also includes time tested formulas for mixing your own greenhouse and nursery soil—thereby helping to provide one of the essential ingredients needed for plant production.

The most important part of your introduction to career opportunities in horticulture will consist of a series of practical field studies. These exercises provided in *Plants for Profit* will help you not only to evaluate real businesses and institutions in operation, but also to recognize the many other facets of commercial horticulture which might prove interesting and profitable.

Most people benefit more through these self-directed studies than could be accomplished by hundreds of hours of classroom courses. The obvious care and remarkable insight which "ordinary" people display while completing these field studies far outshines the effort most university students put forth during formal training for this subject.

At the end of *Plants for Profit* you can find other books listed which will lead you into more specific areas of commercial horticulture. These references may be available at your local library or bookstores, on the internet at *www.andmar.com,* or by mail-order using the order blanks provided.

Over the years I have sold millions of plants, trees,

and flowers. This business has not only been profitable for me—it has also provided an interesting, healthful, and fulfilling career which I would not trade for any other.

Do you want to enjoy the same benefits? If so, then get busy gathering the information and making the decisions necessary to assure success. Many years ago I had a pleasant and secure job as a university professor—it wasn't easy to give up that good life for an uncertain future as a horticultural grower. But the choice has proven to be both a spiritual and monetary "goldmine." Your career can be as equally rewarding.

PART I

STARTING AND OPERATING A HORTICULTURAL BUSINESS

Chapter 1

BUSINESS AND MARKETING HIGHLIGHTS

Many people get ahead financially in life because they purposely choose an expanding career field which offers exceptional opportunity. I have always known that my choice of a business in ornamental horticulture was a lucky one—but only a few days ago this fact was demonstrated more forcefully than ever.

The financial segment of network news listed some of the most dynamic and profitable industries of the 1980's and 90's—as expected, computer technology, pharmaceuticals, and marquee industries were high on the list. But guess which field was expanding more quickly than any other? Yes, it was gardening—over 59% in the past 5 years!

It might seem that even a fool could make good money in such a booming field. However, I can guarantee that making a super income has not been a cakewalk for me. Even with a good deal of luck, there are many things a person must learn before they can expect to receive

$100,000 or more per year. Yes, you may make a few thousand quite easily—but no one I know in this industry really prospers financially unless they operate in a businesslike and knowledgeable manner.

That's what *Plants For Profit* is all about. It gives you a detailed list of general business, marketing, and growing pointers which can help you make a generous income. These pointers may even be used by persons who are not quite so ambitious. If you only want to make $10,000 per year in extra income—why not do it more easily and surely by learning where the opportunities and pitfalls lie? I can save you a lot of time, money, and heartache, but you must be willing to give freely of your energy and attention. This book will not only get you started quickly in the right direction, it will show you how to find further information about specific details.

Ornamental horticulture is a booming industry—and changes are taking place quickly. There are more opportunities in this business than ever before, but you must have a realistic strategy for accomplishing your goals. Nothing is more important when developing a valid business strategy than to realize that no "one-size-fits-all" plan is applicable to every business operation.

You must have some idea of how the ornamental plant industry is structured in order to develop a business plan. At the present time, about one half of the plant merchandise is supplied by relatively large growers and is sold through mass market retail outlets (supermarkets, discount stores, hardware chains, etc.). Another one half of crops are produced by small to medium size growers who sell primarily through their own retail outlet or other independent garden stores. Although there are many possible intermediate situations, the industry is generally divided into big operators and small operators. This is not to say that the big boys are the ones who make the best money—in fact (from my experience), they often receive the lowest profits.

The point I want to emphasize is that there is good money to be made whether you choose to run a large volume operation or a more moderate-sized business. But choose you must—because the same business plan and operational methods cannot be used for both situations.

I generally counsel people who ask my advice that they should begin growing plants in a step-wise fashion. That is, to devise a business plan which allows them to complete one stage in a profitable fashion before beginning the next step. And I usually point out that the great majority of successful businesses in this field are smaller or medium sized operations which are carefully and knowledgeably managed by their owners. Many of the larger operations are inefficiently managed and simply trade dollars from one hand to the other.

My suggestion for you is to initially aim towards starting a rather small plant business, and carefully expand as circumstances warrant until you reach an income range which satisfies your appetite. In no case should you leap into a large scale enterprise with the hope of making millions of dollars within a short time. Millions can be made, but only if you acquire the necessary knowledge and develop a realistic plan of action to reach that goal. And only if you are willing to endure all the sacrifices necessary for such lofty success.

Great success usually entails great risk. My personal business philosophy has always been to pursue a generous income level, but one which requires only a slight amount of financial risk. After all, this is what business is all about—making money surely and reliably, not gambling with wild schemes! The following discussion will emphasize those points which I have found most important in operating a successful family-owned plant business. Please interpret the information presented in that light. Most of the points are equally applicable, with some modification, to larger businesses.

A big question which you should begin considering right now is: "Am I really inclined towards and capable of being a business person?" This chapter may help you find the answer, or at least come closer. Many people never resolve this question fully, and, as a result, cause themselves untold heartache. A committed businessperson who enters the field after serious soul searching and technical preparation seldom fails. But if your main objective is to simply spend time enjoying plants, you should forget about making money and pursue your interests only as a hobby.

We should consider one final topic. Exactly what do I mean when I say "Make $100,000 And More Growing Plants, Trees, And Flowers." Does this figure represent salary, sales, or profit? For the present purposes, this amount represents the combined salary and profit which one hard working and knowledgeable person might expect from a successful plant growing and selling business. If your spouse helps out, you might expect more. Some businesses may yield $100,000 profit after a reasonable owner's salary is deducted, but this is harder to achieve. My statement about $100,000 has nothing to do with gross sales—it is possible to sell a million dollars worth of plants and still wind up losing money!

The following pointers are meant to be brief—a long elaboration of each would prevent you from getting a quick overview of business principles. If you wish to study particular topics in more detail, obtain copies of the following books: *How to Make Money Growing Plants, Trees, and Flowers* and *The Greenhouse And Nursery Handbook.* Details are available in the resource section at the end of this book.

BUSINESS PLAN ESSENTIAL

After deciding to start a horticultural business, you need to construct a blueprint of how this feat will be accomplished. This may seem quite obvious, but it is surprising how many people simply jump in and start without any firm idea about how they will proceed and where they are going. Even fewer develop their plans in detail or formally record them for future reference.

Writing down a detailed business strategy forces you to organize and evaluate all the preliminary thoughts which have popped into mind. During this process, you will most likely find that some ideas, when considered more carefully, do not look so good or conflict with other goals. This is the purpose of a business plan—to organize, clarify, and formalize the process which you will use to become successful. The final plan should provide a logical, step-by-step road map which helps you navigate through all the decisions which will have to be made in the future.

A business plan should not be too brief or exceedingly detailed. A very general plan is too vague to be of much use while complex plans are too rigid and will need to be constantly modified when unforeseen situations arise.

Try to strike a happy medium when the business strategy is formally written down for future reference.

The following points will help you get a better idea of how to construct a business plan. Certain categories may be added or deleted, depending upon special circumstances.

What are your goals?

- Exactly what kind of business do you want to create? Retail? Wholesale? Combination? Service Business?, etc.
- Are certain values more important than profit in your business philosophy?
- How do you want the community to envision you and your company?
- Can you write a clear statement of your business goals in 25 words or less?

Factors influencing your business

- List the three main positive strengths your firm will possess.
- List the three main weaknesses which may hinder your firm's progress.
- What will make your business special in terms of competitive advantages?
- Where can you get reliable information upon which to base business decisions?
- What financial resources do you have now? Are there future possibilities of access to capital?
- What other concrete resources do you possess (land, education, health, buildings, vehicles, etc.)?
- List the specific group or groups of customers you expect to have as a clientele.
- How is the general business climate in your location? Do you have serious competition for your chosen customer base?
- Who will staff your new business? Are the people available for primary positions capable and well-versed for their responsibilities?
- Is your family behind you?

- Are there any serious risk factors which may endanger your venture?

Strategy

- How do you plan to capitalize upon the strengths and de-emphasize the weaknesses of your firm?
- What is the time frame allowed for accomplishing your overall goals?
- List the three fundamental aspects of your business which must guide every decision you make (examples might be: customer service, product quality, profit, risk).
- Define how much capital and work you are willing to put forth. Have you set limits on the amount of risk to be tolerated?
- What percentage of monetary return is acceptable to you as reward for your investment in work and capital? Be sure to arrive at a numeric value.
- Do you have a formalized long range marketing plan? Does it include specific numerical projections?
- Do you have a formalized long range production plan? Does it include specific numerical projections?
- What is your overall plan for fulfilling labor needs?
- Do your personal expectations and aspirations coincide with business goals?

Getting things done

- How is each particular goal or strategic objective to be reached? Write a short synopsis for future reference.
- When will each specific goal be accomplished?
- Who will be responsible for specific goals?
- How much will each objective cost? Set up a budget for every major business category.
- How will you know when each objective is achieved?

Assessment of progress

- Have you reached each objective?
- If not, what is the status?
- Is the direction properly set?
- Should the course of action be changed?
- Should you continue with this project?

- Have conditions changed enough to warrant updating the business plan or completely revising it?

SUCCESS TAKES TIME

Many people start a business with the unrealistic hope of becoming rich overnight. I want to caution that, even in a booming industry like ornamental horticulture, it will generally take 2-5 years before the business becomes truly profitable. You may find that the seed money used to start up and a reasonable owner's wage can be paid out earlier, but don't count on any extra profits for a few years. This is one of the main reasons why start up businesses fail—they did not budget properly for the extended time it usually takes to get off the ground.

I'm not saying success can't come very quickly if you hit some lucky circumstances, but it is safer to expect a few bumps in the road before reaching your final destination. Most business persons find that they become successful by adding small profit centers over the years. It takes time to discover and implement money making programs—but the end result is well worth the effort.

One good way to assure financial success and make it happen sooner is to develop habits of thought and action which inevitably lead toward that goal. A few individuals are naturally talented in this respect, but most people (including myself) must learn these habits through hard experience or through the counsel of others.

An outline of the horticultural success factors which I have found to be most important will soon be provided—please read over this outline several times. And then repeat this process every week during the next 6 months. Hopefully, this repetitive exercise will permanently implant each success factor in your mind. You can then begin to grow and sell plants successfully, as if it were second nature—easily making the proper decisions because your brain is trained to methodically evaluate each new situation.

WHAT IS NOT NECESSARY

Before getting into those factors which are required for success in horticultural business, let's consider some things which are only marginally important. Although some of these items may confer a slight advantage, they certainly are not essential in most cases.

- College degree—Advanced science and business courses may help, but a sound primary education in reading, writing, and arithmetic is the only background you need for success. All the specific information necessary is readily available if you possess these basic skills.
- High intelligence—Of course it helps to possess great mental ability, but this is only one of many characteristics which will determine your success. Patience, perseverance, personality, communication skills, personal health, and numerous other factors are just as important.
- Computer literacy—Most small or medium size horticultural businesses have almost no real need of computer applications. If there is a specific need, it can often be performed more efficiently by hiring the work out to a specialist.
- Fancy facilities—One of the most common mistakes beginners in this business make is to build larger or more sophisticated facilities than can be profitably employed at the time. Usable, efficient facilities are important, but they need not be fancy or expensive.
- Special location—Choose your business location carefully, but don't pay a fortune for characteristics which are not specifically important to your type of horticultural business. Most plant based facilities do not require a high traffic count— in fact, customers may prefer a more sedate atmosphere. Research your needs diligently and use common sense to make this important decision. Don't rely upon a real estate sales person who probably knows little about horticulture or

business to help you select the proper location.
- Luck—If you stay in business over a period of years, you will get a share of bad and good luck. It will all even out over the long run. Therefore, your lasting success will be determined by sound business practices rather than the effect of random events over which you have no control.
- New fangled equipment—You must have equipment capable of performing the job at hand. But this doesn't mean it must be new, expensive, or on the cutting edge of technology. In fact, I have generally found it pays not to purchase new technology until several years after it is introduced—when all the bugs have been worked out.
- Cut throat or deceptive business practices—Business owners must take advantage of every opportunity to gain an honest, competitive edge. This sometimes means your adversaries may suffer to some degree. But don't use dishonest means to accomplish objectives, always treat customers and fellow business persons with the same degree of human respect you desire. By acting in this manner, you will gain the respect of everyone. Horticulture is a field in which trust plays a large part, don't neglect to cultivate this virtue in your dealings.
- Perpetual work—Few people get ahead in business without hard work. However, don't go to the extreme of working to exhaustion. It is not good for your health, and it seldom leads to lasting financial success. You need time to think about and organize business programs—this cannot be done properly if you are continually dead-tired.
- Space age information—Most of the information you need for success has been around for years. It must simply be gathered up, organized, and employed properly. In fact, I usually prefer not to use some of the newest information until more daring souls have tried it and shown whether or not it possesses any value. In most cases, new information has little practical application until all the kinks have been worked out.
- Large operation—It is not necessary to have a big operation to be financially successful in horticulture. Sometimes it doesn't hurt to be big, but the most consistently successful people I meet in this industry are those who concentrate upon selling a reasonable amount of product at the highest possible

price. This means they are market-oriented and market wise. They grow crops which are in demand, and they set their prices at a level which will yield a good profit—then they work hard at devising programs to effectively sell at their established price.

* Good-Old-Boy network—Many people think that success can be achieved only through the established network which exists in any field of endeavor. This method of operation leads generally to mediocrity. How can you consistently come up with new programs and new ideas if you are burdened with old taboos and established methods handed down by generation after generation of old fogies? You should gather the best ideas from all sources, then try them without regard to whether or not some supposed authority says they will work.

LIST OF SUCCESS POINTERS

The success factors listed below are based primarily upon my personal experience in horticultural business. Other persons might add a few points or delete some—but most growers who have been successful would likely give you the same basic advice. Many of the success pointers relate to almost any business field, while certain ones apply specifically to horticulture. Some of the pointers are more important than others because they cover a greater variety of applications. Be sure to keep an eye out for the ones you feel are most useful for your circumstances. See if you can think of any that may be accidentally left out.

Every success factor is not easily categorized. In other words, it is not always readily distinguished from others that are closely related. Don't worry about this; it doesn't matter whether a point is listed in one category or the other, as long as you understand the meaning.

A lot more could be said now about each topic, but doing so would defeat the main purpose of providing an easily remembered basic outline. Much more will be provided later. Consult the ending resource guides for more detailed knowledge about specific topics.

General business pointers

- Make sure you definitely want to own a business. Some people are not cut out to work for themselves—always remember, there is a financial risk involved. Then make sure you possess both the capabilities and resources to become successful. Look at several different business fields in which you have an interest, make a final choice based upon both interest and financial regards.
- Don't count on getting rich fast. Most businesses take several years to become profitable.
- Construct a formal business plan. Write down the main points for future reference.
- Be sure your interest in the field chosen is likely to be enduring. Don't make up your mind too quickly, wait a few months before committing to any important steps. If you can't be enthusiastic about getting into business, even when serious obstacles arise, then it may be the wrong choice for you.
- Be realistic. Go over your plans carefully to make sure you are not being overly optimistic. See if there are any parts of your plan which can be confirmed with actual data. Ask persons (other than friends or relatives) to evaluate your plans, then listen carefully to what they tell you.
- Knowledge is the key to success. Make sure you learn everything possible about the chosen business. Don't skimp on resources which will increase your knowledge. One $20 book may contain information which eventually is worth thousands of dollars. You never know when or where you will discover important concepts which can transform your financial life, so be serious about pursuing an educational program. Take field trips, investigate the competition, read books, ask questions—this is the way you become truly successful.
- Set goals you expect to attain within definite time frames, and then give yourself predetermined rewards for reaching

each important step. This process allows you to enjoy the fruits of success rather than falling into a mind-numbing routine of more and more work which has no visible purpose.

- Take time to think through and plan your business programs. A little advance planning can eliminate a lot of unnecessary work.

- Planning and action must be carefully balanced. Too much or too little of either can be bad.

- Place a realistic value upon your time. Then evaluate all business programs upon the basis of how much of your time they require. This process will help you allocate more time to the most productive programs and less to those which are not so efficient.

- Every business program must make sense. Periodically evaluate everything you do to make sure it makes a profit or has other redeeming characteristics. Discard those programs which no longer or never did have any substantial basis for existence.

- Periodically make sure you are on the right track. Sometimes it is easy to become distracted by unimportant things and lose sight of major goals. Stand back and take an overall look at your business at least once a year—see if it is headed in the right direction. Prioritize your time and major projects to make certain they agree with the direction you want the company to take.

- Learn to tackle one project or problem at a time. Sticking religiously to this rule may not be practical in many cases, but try to follow it as much as possible. Juggling several projects at once usually dilutes your attention and may lead to shoddy work or poor decisions. It can also make you a nervous wreck. List projects or problems in order of priority and work on each in sequence; you will be surprised how fast the list dwindles as you efficiently finish each task. Work goes quickly when you can concentrate on one thing at a time.

- Quantify whenever possible. Try to express yourself in numerical form; this is usually a more precise means of communication than are words—especially in business applications. Examine every aspect of your information and then devise means of assigning numbers to it when possible.

If you think hard, it may be surprising how much information expressed as words can be converted to a numerical representation. It gets easier to do each time you practice. For example, instead of saying "we intend to grow a lot of Maple trees and less of Oak and Ash", say "we intend to grow 50% Maple trees, 30% Oak and 20% Ash".

- Be versatile: react quickly to new circumstances. One of the chief advantages small businesses have over larger competitors is the ability to adapt more quickly to changing or newly emerging conditions. This capacity should be built into your various business programs.
- Learn from others. Observe how your competitors and other types of businesses operate. Copy their successful programs. Even those who are failures probably have one or two good points you can use to your advantage.
- Pay attention to hunches. Intuitive flashes usually occur after a long build up of information in your mind reaches a critical stage. At this point, answers to previously baffling problems may surface instantaneously without conscious effort. Most business decisions should be made through logical thought processes, but there are times when intuition helps you make a final choice.
- Don't confuse gambling with business. Eliminating risk is one of the major objectives in business; this is how you build a solid predictable income flow over which you possess a good deal of control. Gambling is subject to the laws of chance over which you have absolutely no control. Evaluate every business program from the standpoint of how much risk it involves; when the risk becomes too great, then you are entering the realm of gambling, rather than practicing sound business principles.
- Be aware of your financial condition. Know at all times how profitable your business is, how much ready cash is available, and what financial obligations exist. This doesn't mean you must keep track of every penny, but you should constantly have valid approximations of these facts in mind. A more accurate accounting should be made at least twice a year.
- Don't overextend yourself financially. Many people fail at business because they do not know what their financial

condition is, or because they know but have never learned to live within a realistic budget. Long term business success requires that you be reasonably conservative with expenses. Maintain a sufficient emergency fund; some businesses thrive during good times but go under at the first hint of adversity because no back up funds are available for the lean times which arise from time to time.

- Evaluate the major needs of your business and make sure they are adequately funded before spending money on less important aspects. Don't skimp or be cheap on essential long term facilities, machinery, or services—if you must economize, do it on less critical needs or ones that do not have long term implications. If the budget plan shows you cannot afford to take care of the major needs adequately, develop an alternate business strategy which is more in line with available funds.

- Businesses have different needs at different stages of development. So do the people who own them. Evaluate your company and personal life periodically to make sure policies and programs are meeting current requirements.

- Some small businesses are highly profitable but don't do so well when they are expanded. This may be because the business simply isn't adaptable to a larger scene or perhaps the wrong methods are used during and on completion of the expansion.

- Be certain to collect all the money that is due to you. This seems like an obvious necessity but many businesses fail simply because they neglect to make sure customers pay on time in full. I find that customers often cease to do business with me when I let them get behind. They become embarrassed at their situation and try to avoid contact.

Marketing pointers

- Every business owner must be market and customer oriented—this is the first priority. No business can succeed without a profitable market for products or services. Production must be dictated by marketing efforts, not vice versa. Persons who grow plants often get the sequence backwards, they produce crops and then try to market them.

This is all wrong! It leads to more failures and low profit situations amongst horticulturists than any other cause.

- Listen to the customer. Allow customers to show by their purchases which plants, trees, and flowers they like best. Devise marketing programs by which you can test customer preferences before full scale production is started. Don't risk extensive crop production until market testing has shown that consumers will purchase your plants at a price which provides an acceptable profit. Market testing is basically simple—it means that you offer plants for sale at particular prices and then determine how well they sold at each test price.

- Know your customers. This doesn't mean you need to know them personally, but you do need to understand what types of plants and flowers they prefer, how much they are willing to pay, when they are likely to buy, and a number of other basic customer characteristics which will vitally affect business decisions.

- Repeat business is critical to a successful business operation. Customers will not return if your trees, plants, and flowers do not perform acceptably. And they will not return unless you provide good, courteous service. It costs money to find customers; in order to recover your investment in them it is important they return in the future. Satisfied customers are like money in the bank. The primary marketing advantage an informed horticulturist has over mass merchant outlets is in helping customers choose proper plant varieties for climatic conditions and specific uses. Providing detailed instructions for care after the purchase is also an important component of long term success.

- Guarantee all plants, trees, and flowers. This doesn't mean you must guarantee them under all conditions, but they must meet your customers' expectations of a fair deal. Trust is a very important ingredient in the success of any horticultural business. Don't argue with customers about the details of a guarantee—no guarantee at all is better than one that is honored grudgingly. Price your plants so that they reflect the cost of a guarantee.

- Believe in yourself, your products and services. It is impossible to present a positive image to customers if you can't even convince yourself that plants, trees, and flowers are worth the asking price. You must believe that horticultural products are an important aspect of our cultural and biological life. It is much easier to have pride in your work if you aim at the high end of the market which appreciates beautiful plants, rather than the low end where price is the main consideration.

- Know the competition, but don't let it dictate your policies. Many producers of ornamental plants fail to realize good profits because they consistently base decisions upon what the competition is doing. Price your merchandise on the basis of what is needed for a decent profit rather than upon how much everyone else is charging. I always check out major competitors for prices, quality, and new items, but then I try to see how I can put my company in a position of leadership rather than following everyone else.

- Know how the selling price of merchandise affects profits and other aspects of your business. You can sell a mountain of merchandise and still lose money. Many plant producers fail to understand the tremendous impact a few cents difference in price can have on profits. This is especially noticeable if you operate near the break-even point. It is easy to construct numerical charts for each product which graphically illustrate how profits are affected at different levels of price and volume. Analyzing your business in this manner can often lead to thousands of dollars in increased profits very quickly. Numerous factors such as competition, product availability and cost, demand and quality, must enter into price calculations. Although price is important, it may not be the main factor which determines business success. In horticulture, such things as quality, availability and selection are often more critical.

- **Don't advertise commercially more than necessary.** Advertising is generally very costly, and it doesn't add one bit to the quality or usefulness of your plants, trees, and flowers. Most horticultural operations derive the majority of sales from word of mouth referrals—therefore, it makes good sense to be sure every customer who comes in is well-satisfied with the service and products. This satisfied customer will then recommend you to a relative or friend—the process goes on and on. While a certain amount of conventional advertising may be productive, the majority of effort and expense should be aimed at offering superior plants and service which will produce enthusiastic recommendations from people who purchase them.

- Develop all possible profit centers. By this, I mean that you should look for and actively develop all the means of making money that exist within your business. If you think carefully, there may be several good money making projects that have been neglected. Scarcely a year passes in which I don't discover a new profit program that has escaped my previous attention. As the years pass, numerous small profit centers can add up to a very significant income.

- Integrate your horticultural business vertically. A vertically integrated business is one in which the company participates in several activities which could be handled separately by different companies. In horticultural business, it normally means that you both grow and sell your own plants. The extra activities included allow your company to make more profit while handling the same amount of merchandise. Even more activities than growing and selling can be easily included—such as manufacturing your own soil, or producing your own small starter plants.

Plant Growing Pointers

- Growing plants, trees, and flowers is profitable only if you have a carefully constructed production plan. This plan should contain a logical program for each major aspect of the growing operation. Examples of the programs which might be included are: A) facilities, B) labor, C) machinery, D) environmental factors such as soil, water, fertilizer, temperature, light, etc., E) crop and variety selection, F) insect and disease control, G) marketing and economic analysis, H) crop scheduling. Every individual program which is developed must integrate successfully with all other programs contained in the overall production plan. Each program and the overall plan should be systematized so that commercial crops can be reliably and profitably produced on a regular basis.

- There must be a profitable market available for every crop you grow. Don't produce plants on a speculative basis—you should have a definite marketing plan in place before any crop is started. More profit is possible if you identify major marketing trends, and then produce crops which fit in with these trends—in other words, "go with the flow".
- Each new crop of plants, trees, or flowers should be grown first on a test basis (preferably, more than one time). Full production runs often cost a good deal of money; there is no sense in risking full production until the crop has a proven market and the cultural details have been worked out. Variations in local climate from year to year can often cause unforeseen difficulties in plant growth. Even if a particular crop looks promising on paper, you will be lucky if 1 in 4 is ultimately profitable over the long run. Each new crop is a gamble and should be phased in gradually.
- Be patient. The necessity to test crops and phase them in gradually requires patience, but it is the only prudent way to operate. You must also bide your time as crops are growing—there is seldom any means of speeding up normal growth appreciably without adversely affecting plant quality. You cannot hurry Mother Nature: she takes her own sweet time, and we mortals must learn to live with it.
- Timing of crops for market is critical. In order to make the best profit (or any profit at all!) most ornamentals must be marketed within definite time frames. These marketing periods may be dictated by calendar holidays, seasonal factors, or climatic variations. Meticulous advance planning and crop scheduling are the most important means of assuring that crops will be ready at the opportune marketing time. However, minor manipulation of crop culture and environment may also be practiced upon occasion. Growers must be on top of the scheduling problem for every crop at all times.
- Learn to deal with rush periods. Since most ornamental plants, trees, and flowers are sold within rather short time periods, you must be willing to work hard at peak seasons of planting, harvesting, and selling. Failure to do so often results in lost market share and a decline of product quality. Plants, trees, and flowers are perishable. Every business that handles or

grows them must place a good deal of emphasis upon inventory control. Careful attention should be focused upon providing the proper amounts of suitable quality at exactly the right time. This is not an easy task. Inventory control is mainly exercised through advance planning of crops and marketing. However, a small amount of control can be accomplished through minor adjustments of crop culture and marketing as the harvest period approaches or is in progress. Failure to implement strict inventory control causes excessive dumping of crops. It is not hard to see how "dumpage" can quickly lead to an unprofitable operation.

- Accept crop and marketing failures as part of life. Given the many variables which can affect crop culture and sales, it is inevitable that occasional failures will arise—put these unfortunate incidents on the compost pile and go on to the next task. Many people never learn this important lesson, and, as a consequence, they gradually accumulate entire fields or greenhouses full of old and useless plants that consume valuable working time just to maintain. These useless stockpiles frequently become breeding grounds for diseases and insects which infect new crops. Although you must learn to deal with failure, do not become nonchalant about it— take every reasonable step to prevent a similar occurrence in the future. Learn from your mistakes!

- Be aware of crop production expenses. Knowing how much a particular plant, flower, or tree will cost to produce is the initial step in understanding what the selling price must be. Accurate calculation of production costs for a crop can sometimes become complex—but it must be done if you are to have any realistic basis for profit objectives. Dependable expense and crop records are essential for determining how much it costs to produce individual crops—you cannot simply pull the figures out of the air. Although published industry expense averages may be interesting for comparison purposes, they cannot be relied upon for pricing purposes in actual practice. There is too much variation from region to region and grower to grower for these estimates to be valid. Every plant, tree, and flower requires time and a space in which to grow. The profits of a commercial horticulturist depend, to a large extent, upon the costs involved in providing this space and time. Each crop must be evaluated upon the basis of how long it will occupy a particular unit of space. This is the only way you can arrive at a valid pricing schedule which definitely yields a profit. The exact means of calculating these figures is completely explained in *The Greenhouse And Nursery Handbook.*

- Learn to interact with employees in a productive manner. Most business owners rate labor-related factors as their biggest problem. The production of ornamental plants, trees, and flowers is generally labor intensive—this means that labor management must be a top priority. If you are the only worker, it is even more important to work efficiently. Labor is almost always the largest expense in crop production and marketing. Therefore, it is likely to be a very important determinant of company profitability. Labor costs must be kept within a range that allows you to produce a competitive crop. Much of this objective can be met through effective labor management, but a good part of it must be accomplished through keeping a lid on wages. Poor communication between managers and workers is often a major reason why productivity is low—this problem is the manager's responsibility, not the employee's. You must look upon employees not only as the largest expense, but also as the company's most valuable asset—don't jeopardize the entire organization through haphazard, uninformed, or contentious labor management.

- Provide workers with proper facilities, tools, and instruction for the job. Since labor will likely be the biggest expense of growing plants, trees, and flowers, you should get the most out of every hour. This doesn't mean all the facilities or tools must be new or expensive—simply adequate. Proper instruction about tasks is even more important—and this doesn't cost a dime. One well-trained employee can do the work of 3 or 4 who are poorly prepared. Written work orders are a good way to ensure that jobs are done correctly and completely.

- Horticultural businesses are often highly seasonal. Your labor management plan should carefully take this variable work load into account. It can become a major problem if it is not given advance consideration. Try to make seasonal workers reasonably permanent from year to year by hiring people who can accept and may even prefer this type of work. Neighborhood homemakers and retired persons are perhaps the most dependable and productive help in this regard. Some high school and college students may also be used if they display a mature work attitude.

- Don't over invest in facilities or machines which are marginally useful to your business. Many people go machine "crazy" and purchase more than can be profitably used. Unless a machine or facility is utilized consistently, it often makes more sense to handle the task by temporarily increasing the labor force. Remember, a worker can be laid off or dismissed when the job ends—a machine costs money whether it is working or not. And machines sometimes become obsolete quickly. Machines are also generally rather restricted in what they can do—people are much more flexible. Consider your purchases of facilities and equipment carefully; be sure they make sense from a profit standpoint.

- Visit other growing establishments and copy their best ideas. At least once a year you should spend a few days checking out new possibilities for your business. Only one good idea could be worth thousands of dollars in increased production, sales, or expenses saved. Don't adopt every new thing you see. Check it out carefully first to make sure it fits into your organization and will actually turn a profit. You should easily be able to find one good new plant or money saving method each year that will increase profits by $500.00. In the course of 30 years in business, this would add $15,000.00 net income per year.

- The majority of crops should generally consist of proven "bread and butter" items which have substantial demand. You can make more money by slightly improving a popular high volume crop than by introducing a new crop for which there is limited demand. Developing new methods of using popular plants, trees, and flowers is also a good means of increasing profits dramatically. Several economic characteristics of each crop should be analyzed on a regular basis. In addition to space, time, and total growing expenses mentioned above, you must keep track of how well crops sell under "real time" situations, what the sales trends indicate (up, down, or sideways), and how crop profitability compares with existing or potential competing crops. You need to perform a comprehensive evaluation of which plants will provide your operation with the greatest profit. After all, there are thousands of varieties you could be growing—your job is to concentrate upon those which will make the most money under the existing circumstances.

- Insects, diseases, and other pests are a major and continuing problem in any horticultural business. They must be effectively and economically controlled if you expect to run a profitable operation. Pest control should be dealt with in a thorough, logical, and continuing manner if it is to be successful. Haphazard methods will not work. Whatever means you choose to employ should be carefully evaluated for human and environmental safety as well as for effectiveness and economy. There are numerous federal and state laws which regulate the use of pesticides—be sure you are aware of the ones which apply to your operation.

- All businesses that grow plants, trees, and flowers are affected by weather and climate. Although you can't do anything about the weather, you can prepare for its ramifications through advance planning. Weather also greatly influences the marketing of horticultural crops. Therefore, it is absolutely essential that you carefully consider weather factors whenever any business program is being planned or evaluated. The weather can sometimes control every aspect of a horticultural business. You must know the climate as well as possible, plan for it and, in the end, accept it.

- Plant growing businesses exhibit several general methods of operation. The different methods often grade into one another in actual practice so that most businesses are hybrid combinations. 1) Specialist grower—tends to restrict activities to a particular crop (such as bedding plants), or to a specific step in crop production (such as propagation). 2) Diversified grower—grows several different crops and often performs at least several critical steps in the growing process. 3) Vertically integrated grower—strives to perform as many operations and grow as many crops as is practically possible within a single organization. Somewhat different than the diversified grower in that the emphasis is upon self-contained operation rather than total crop diversification. 4) Wholesale grower—serves as a wholesale source for retail outlets. May or may not participate in retail activities themselves. 5) Retail grower—grows plants for and sells plants directly to the retail consumer.

Chapter 2

HOW AND WHERE TO GET FINANCING FOR A HORTICULTURAL BUSINESS

Money is the universal lubricant of business. It makes all the parts work well together when it is applied in the proper places, at the proper time, and in the right amounts. Many inexperienced persons have the idea that business can be carried on more successfully as increasing amounts of money are added. Nothing could be further from the truth. The failure of numerous businesses can be traced to the inappropriate and untimely use of more money than is required by circumstances.

My purpose in this chapter is not only to suggest ways and places to obtain money for your horticultural business, but also to briefly point out how it may be used wisely.

Your effort to use money for making more money will be doomed to failure unless you carry out the second step of the equation as successfully as the first.

In general, various topics about how to obtain funds by borrowing or related means will be discussed. Less frequently, money sources which do not require repayment (the latter are understandably more rare in occurrence) will be mentioned.

I'm sure that most readers already realize (at least in a vague way) that borrowing or using someone elses' funds is going to cost money. The reason I mention this fact is that many people have a predisposition to ignore the horrible news unless it stares them directly in the face. Another reason for emphasizing this is the common practice of lenders to gloss over the often outrageous costs associated with loan repayment. Get this basic lesson firmly planted in your head right now—people generally expect to be paid handsomely for letting you use their money. After all, it is perhaps their most prized possession!

Although borrowing or using other peoples' money entails some risk and significant costs, almost everyone engages in it. Why so? Because the borrower expects to enjoy certain benefits from using these funds. When borrowing for business use, you presumably expect to make a profit greater than the loan cost, or, perhaps, you will be able to get started on a long term project sooner than if you slowly saved all the necessary funds. Be sure you always carefully examine whether the hoped for benefits will significantly outweigh the cost of capital.

A caution about borrowing has been raised now so that you will hopefully interpret the remaining information with a sober eye—unwise or uninformed borrowing is at the root of many problems in society and is the cause of untold personal misery. Be sure you are fully appraised of the downside aspects you may encounter when making use of loans or related financial vehicles.

Now that the proper cautions have been posted, it is only reasonable to tell you that most successful businesses are built upon some form of borrowed capital. You are more likely to amass a fortune and to do it more quickly if you make use of the additional funds someone else can supply.

Many, perhaps most, businesses would never be started if borrowed capital were not available. In addition to making things happen more surely and quickly, extra money can also make things easier for the budding entrepreneur. Money enables us to purchase and make use of many modern conveniences such as machines, labor, information, etc. Borrowed money can help make your life easier and more prosperous, but be sure you use it in ways which lead to these desirable goals.

SOME COMMENTS ABOUT BUSINESS AND MONEY

Before you seek financing for a new or existing business, there are several points which should be thoroughly considered. Each of them is related in some manner to the subject of "risk." Successful business persons unconsciously endeavor to minimize the risk in every aspect of their venture.

The most useful tool you can possess in order to make a business less risky is a "business plan."

This plan should provide a broad outline of objectives to be reached and the methods that will be used to attain these goals.

Business plans should always start with an overall perspective, and then provide some detail about specific aspects of the outline. How much or how little detail is included depends upon how the plan will be employed. In general, a good deal of detail is necessary when business plans are utilized for evaluating the financial aspects of a business. Basically, you want to construct a hypothetical picture of how profitable your business will be and how and when the money will flow through it. This information allows you to plan ahead for your money needs and for eventual repayment of loans.

I can offer certain other advice about how to reduce the risk as you start up a horticultural business. These points certainly do not cover every specific area but do include the major aspects. My first suggestion for budding horticultural entrepreneurs is always—work for someone else in a similar business before you start your own. This experience is the most valuable tool you can have in planning your own venture, and it will be an important consideration whenever you apply for loans or grants.

Another business strategy I always recommend is to develop a venture in step-wise fashion. In other words, arrange your business start up so that certain critical phases of it are completed and proving profitable before the next stage is begun. This allows you to concentrate capital in specific projects, and it means that money is not being invested in more than one unproven venture at any time. Adopting this one-step-at-a-time strategy can often lower start up costs significantly. I'm sure you can also see how it reduces risk.

In general, extra money can be more effectively and safely used in businesses which have developed successfully past the start up phase. In this stage you usually know whether or not borrowed money can be employed profitably with little risk. Start up ventures often fail within a relatively short time.

This fact should prompt you to ask: Is it prudent to borrow money when first starting a business? The answer is: It depends upon how carefully you have prepared and analyzed a business plan. If a well done plan shows the venture will make money, then borrowing is justified. If the opposite is true, or if you have no organized plans, don't borrow.

You should not gamble with borrowed money. Gambling is permissible only with money you can afford to lose. The business plan you construct and use for predicting future results is the key element which transforms a business start up from pure gambling into a well-calculated and acceptable risk.

We could certainly explore many further aspects of general business theory, but this is not the specific objective of the chapter. Key points have been mentioned because they are especially important to keep in mind as you digest the following information.

MONEY MANAGEMENT TIPS

Borrowing money is serious business. You should manage the funds obtained in a responsible fashion, so that both you and the lender benefit from the transaction. Borrowing without proper guidelines is one of the surest routes to financial ruin. Listed below are a few (not all) important points of which you should take note. Several more management tips are mentioned under the heading of *Analysis and Documentation*.

- Every potential borrower should determine whether there is a more acceptable alternative means of reaching the objective.
- Hard work can often be substituted for at least a portion of the borrowed funds you need.
- Reduce your requirements for borrowed funds to the absolute minimum. Step-wise business start up is one means of doing so. Leasing and renting facilities or equipment instead of

purchasing is another. Careful management of inventory and inventory payment terms can also reduce the amount of money you need.

- Don't borrow money simply because it is available, too much can sometimes be bad—especially for a beginning business.
- Analyze exactly why you need money, what you are going to use it for, and how and when it can be repaid.
- Borrow only when it will be profitable to you. Then use the money for the shortest period of time possible. The cost of money is based upon risk, amount, and time—if you increase any of these factors, the money will cost more.
- Borrow at the right time and place. The price of money varies tremendously with each of these factors. Both can be controlled to some extent if you take the time to become knowledgeable.
- Determine whether your money needs are short term or long term, or a combination of both. The time factor can affect many aspects of cost, availability, repayment, etc.
- There are many different avenues for obtaining loans, grants, or similar financial packages. Investigate availability in your specific area, and pursue the ones most suitable to your purposes and circumstances. The best package for you may be the worst one for the next person.
- Being a borrower requires real discipline. If you cannot be a responsible borrower, don't do it in the first place.
- Every business person should line up a source of emergency credit for unpredictable needs. This source must not be used for ordinary business purposes; it should be firmly reserved for important unusual situations.

ANALYSIS AND DOCUMENTATION

The suggestions listed below are a part of the overall money management you should employ when borrowing, but they fall more specifically into a group of analysis and documentation procedures.

- Take stock of all the resources you possess—both concrete physical items (such as land, home, stocks and bonds, life insurance equity, vehicles)—and implied resources (which may include good credit history, lack of debt, good education, references, friends, family, experience, stability of residence and employment). All of these factors can be important as you apply for loans, grants, and related financial help. Although concrete assets will usually be the most important, there are many situations in which implied assets could be a major factor in your favor.

- The financial statement mentioned earlier in this book will be a big part of your documentation efforts. It should be carefully filled out since it will most likely be used as a basis for loan approval. Giving false information on loan applications is against the law.
- Be aware that money is a commodity just like anything else—it is costing you money. Know the market price and know the potential costs in terms of time, control, and other factors which may be placed upon your activity.
- Project ahead the amounts which you will need within defined time frames. In other words, know how your money will flow through the business.
- You must see enough future cash flow to pay interest and principal plus an eventual profit.
- Evaluate the borrowing contract carefully, even if the agreement is between you and a relative or friend. Plan on sticking to the agreement religiously right from the start. Have a competent lawyer look over major contracts, but don't rely upon the attorney to catch every possible problem; the final responsibility is yours alone. Grant contracts may also have strict guidelines and rules; you should look at these carefully—especially if you are required to sign any legal documents.
- Always document borrowing costs and grants as they may relate to your federal and state taxes. You will need this information in detail.

MONEY SOURCES

The types of money sources and the amounts of funds available will vary with circumstances. Such factors as geography, time, economic conditions, applicant eligibility, and political conditions will all have some effect upon your chances of obtaining loans and grants.

You must survey the possibilities in this regard, and narrow the search down to a manageable number—perhaps 3 or 4 at the outset. Concentrate your efforts upon these few which seem to offer the best prospect of fulfillment. Presenting a well-organized request for loans and grants is often a lot of work — especially if they are directed towards the more bureaucratic channels and if they involve larger sums of money.

The sources of money listed below certainly do not include every possibility but do represent most of the avenues which a person is likely to find available. You will see that certain categories are discussed in greater detail. Generally, these sources deserve greater attention because they represent an acceptable and easily usable pool of funds for a large number of people. There is certainly some personal preference on my part, this does not mean that your experience will yield the same results.

I offer one caution before you proceed further. Please view every advertisement and offer which proclaims **free money** or **fast money** with a careful eye. While some of these offers may indeed have merit, the great majority use these headlines only to get your attention.

Relatives and friends

Aside from personal assets, this is the most common source of start up funds for small business people. It shouldn't be! You may jeopardize close relationships by using friends and relatives as money lenders. Even when the business is a resounding success, and everyone is paid back according to schedule, some strain may be introduced into the relationship. I don't have to tell you what happens if you can't retire the debt as promised.

If you must borrow from family or friends, insist that everything be formally written down just as if you were getting the money from a bank. This will help you make sure there are no misconceptions which will come back to haunt you in the future.

Banks and commercial lenders

A person might think the local bank or savings and loan would be a prime source for small business start up funds. Don't get your hopes up! Unless you have iron clad collateral, some type of government loan guarantee, or you catch them at a weak moment, banks are not likely to take a risk on you. Bankers are very conservative and like to make their money on sure bets. Occasionally some form of lending hysteria (one of which took place in the 1980's and precipitated the great savings and loan scandal) overcomes their caution. But then the easy money usually goes to slick talkers or old school chums, rather than well-intentioned people like you and me.

Banks not only desire collateral, they want you to show a demonstrated ability to repay the loan. Taking possession of your belongings is a messy business (and it may be expensive), and it isn't what they really like to do. They would much rather receive their payments on schedule. So even if you have adequate collateral but cannot show a steady income source adequate to meet monthly loan payments, don't count on getting a loan.

There are of course various other private companies who are in the business of lending money. Some of these are more-or-less on par with banks or credit unions as far as their integrity and amount of interest charged, and most are reliable firms but charge higher rates than banks, while a few private lenders border upon being unscrupulous, at least with regard to the interest charged.

While banks and commercial lenders are not especially receptive to start up business loans, they are extraordinarily receptive to home improvement loans. It may well be that you can obtain financing for certain business-related expenses through a home loan. Most banks are glad to extend credit for recreational greenhouses if the structure meets certain criteria. Improvements for nursery and perennial beds might also be eligible. Loans for small garden type equipment are available not only through the bank, but most all large stores dealing in this type of merchandise have a time payment program which is easy to utilize.

Home improvement and similar type loans are relatively easy to arrange and can take a good deal of the hassle out of getting the money approved for a project. But I must make it clear that providing false information for loan purposes is against the law.

As long as the improvements are made according to specifications in the loan agreement, you will have no problems. But applying for home improvement money, and then using it for totally unrelated purposes, exposes you to legal action by the lender. The improvement must be for a bonafide purpose which the lending agency gives approval. Incidental use later in your home business will not upset them.

There are several types of assets upon which banks or other types of commercial lenders will loan money. Your home, vehicles, major equipment, land, life insurance cash value, stocks, and bonds may be suitable as collateral. This depends upon the policies of the loaning institution.

Guaranteed loans

Because commercial banks and lending institutions are reluctant to supply small business start up money, various government agencies often act as guarantors of these type of loans. You still borrow the money from a local source, but all or part of the loan repayment is guaranteed by government agencies. The Small Business Administration is perhaps the best known of these agencies but there are several other federal programs and numerous individual state and local government counterparts. (State Farm Loan Boards, Community Development Authorities, Federal Loans for Rural Development, etc.)

If you are located in a basically agricultural area, the local county agent can give you a line on various agricultural loan programs offered by state and federal agencies. And in cities there are all types of programs for minorities, disadvantaged persons, and neighborhood improvement. No matter who you are, chances are good that some special program exists to help you get started in business. It is up to you to do the footwork, and locate the specific program which suits your needs best. Seldom does anyone walk up and give you the money, you have to find out where it is and then ask for it.

Since the local bank is often the conduit through which these governmental loans are channeled, the loan department is a good place to visit for preliminary information.

Most of these sponsored loans cost less interest than a similar commercial loan, but they may involve more paperwork since the government is involved.

In the past few years, many communities and counties have become heavily involved in economic development.

Some of them actually make funds available for new and existing businesses, while some may only offer tax breaks, technical information, or low-cost locations. State governments also offer similar programs. If you live in a small town or small state, these programs can sometimes be more easily arranged since you (or your close acquaintances) may actually know people who have a contact with the programs. Personal relations are often important in getting a good break.

Financial grants

Grants are the best financial aid you can receive. As the name implies, you are not required to pay the money back. It is free if you qualify. Needless to say, there is less likelihood of finding a grant than of obtaining a loan.

Many governmental agencies have small business grants available. These grants mainly cultivate opportunity for disadvantaged population groups and individuals. Some grants are awarded with the idea of stimulating new technologies or to support particular industries. At the present time, the ecological movement provides the impetus for a favorable outlook concerning grant availability for horticultural projects.

If you live in an economically depressed area, there may be a good deal of economic development aid available through state and local agencies. These entities are perhaps the best source of grants for the ordinary person who has no special disabilities or needs. Loans through these avenues are even easier to obtain and usually carry a low interest rate. Economic development grants may be used to finance any stage of a business, but they are commonly awarded to help businesses plan the feasibility and marketing of products, or to train and hire local workers for the new enterprise.

As with loans, it is up to you to find out what grants might be available in your area. If you are associated with or know of a particular special interest group, this is a good place to begin inquiring. Your city and state government may have personnel who specialize in helping citizens locate grant sources. The local county agent's office will be able to point you towards possible grant money in the areas of horticulture, agriculture, home economics, education, etc.

Local educational institutions such as community colleges may be able to steer you in the right direction. Most colleges have a grants coordinator, and, while they may specialize in educational matters, it is highly likely they have information pertaining to your needs or can put you in contact with the proper people.

Public libraries usually have a data base which can be accessed to locate available grants. Ask the librarian if you are not familiar with how to use the facilities.

Since a grant provides something of value for free, you can imagine that the competition is often severe and that the people who seek grants are sometimes looking only for a handout. When you apply for a grant, don't act as if you expect a free lunch—show that you are willing to put something into the project. Often times you will be expected to contribute money to match the grant available—if your venture is viable, this should not be objectionable.

Some grants are not worth the effort—particularly ones which require an extensive application process or which place too many restrictions upon your business activity. Be sure to evaluate these conditions, and be certain of your financial obligations to the granting agency. Some grants are called grants but contain contractual obligations which require eventual repayment—in effect being more of a deferred loan.

Partners

People become associated together in business for many reasons, but one of the most common factors bringing business partners together is the need for money. Partners may pool their monetary resources or one may contribute most of the money while the other contributes mainly expertise and time.

Partners in business can be a good source of financial help, but they want something which an ordinary lender does not demand: a part of the business. You should think long and hard before mortgaging the future control of your enterprise. If the primary need is for money, rather than some other valuable asset a partner can bring into the business, I would suggest that you exhaust all other means of financing before becoming involved in co-ownership.

Life insurance, stocks, bonds, retirement accounts

Like many people, you may have assets which can be borrowed against almost automatically—if the assets are in the proper form and in easily accessible accounts.

Many stock and bond brokers will allow you to "margin" (borrow) against your stocks and bonds. This process is usually ridiculously easy. They may also allow you to do the same thing with retirement securities or CDs. In most cases, you can simply sign a "Margin Agreement" (which your brokerage house sends out) and then have the representative place your assets in a special "Margin

Account." It really is that easy if you qualify for such accounts. Your broker can easily tell you the details in 5 minutes over the phone. All brokerage houses differ in their policies somewhat—check out several. You can easily switch your securities from one to another house by simply signing a transfer form.

The argument may be made that if you have extensive stock, bond, and retirement assets—you do not need to borrow money. This may be true to some small extent, but there are many situations in which it is wise to borrow money for good projects rather than doing without, or it may be better to borrow short term rather than selling other assets to provide capital. I have several margin accounts which I can utilize by simply making out a check drawn against the account.

Of course, margin accounts must be used only for good purposes, otherwise you can find yourself in hot water quickly. It is just like overdrawing a checking account. And you should not choose a broker simply because they provide easy access to margin money. A broker should be selected mainly because they offer the best services related to investment vehicles. You must understand that when borrowing against securities, the money is coming out of your portfolio—which will be worth less until you replace the borrowed amount. And the broker is charging interest on every dollar he loans you.

Margin accounts should be utilized only by persons who are sophisticated enough financially to use them safely. It takes discipline to properly loan yourself money by making out margin checks.

Retirement accounts and life insurance equity are assets which can be easily used as loan collateral. Your banker or stockbroker can tell you quickly how to borrow against retirement accounts. Life insurance loans can be made through the bank or directly with the insurance representative. The cash value or loan value of insurance policies at various prescribed dates is usually found in tables which accompany your policy.

Credit from suppliers

In my estimation, supplier credit is the most useful, most economical, and easiest way to obtain financing for your business. Suppliers are eager to sell you products and they normally have a ready made line of credit if you have a good personal credit history and comply with minimal credit application procedures. Many suppliers will rely upon their personal evaluation of you if you visit them beforehand.

Remember, every supplier has competitors to worry about. If one company won't extend credit, ask another until you find someone who is more eager to do business. Credit policies vary greatly from one supplier to another. Some will give you the fifth degree, while others will allow you to charge with little more than a short personal visit.

The best way to obtain supplier credit is to prepare a credit history and obtain references from your bankers and other credible people who know you. Then arrange a personal interview with the supplier—this face to face encounter is important. It is easy to say "no" over the phone, but, unless there are compelling reasons, the answer will be "yes" in person.

If you are going into business, start developing supplier credit 6 months ahead. Visiting with the company's salesman is a good start; he or she is always anxious to find a new customer. Talk over your plans with salespersons and ask their advice. You will often learn new things about the field, and, even if you don't, the salesperson is the first step towards obtaining credit, sometimes it is the only one necessary.

Starting early allows you to make a few small orders on credit and then pay for them on time—this may be slightly inconvenient, but it establishes your credit record with the company before you need to purchase supplies worth thousands of dollars. Chances are that with 3 or 4 previous purchases you can develop an almost unlimited credit line before you really need it.

As you develop a larger number of supplier credit accounts, it is not difficult to see that you could have the equivalent of a $100,000 loan which is interest free. By working your inventory carefully, you may not require money from other sources. Many larger horticultural companies sometimes have a $100,000 credit line with only one particular supplier and similar credit with several others. Even if you have only a small business to start you can see that a $1,000 to $5,000 credit line would not be considered unusual at a supply house.

Most suppliers have a net 30 days credit policy. This means that you have 30 days from the date of shipping until payment must be made. In many cases, this payment period may be extended to 60 or 90 days. In the agricultural and horticultural industry, it is not unusual for terms to be extended to cover the entire growing and marketing season—this may be 6 months or longer. Be sure to ask your suppliers about their "time dated terms" or "growing season terms." Not all will have them but a large number do.

Of course, the supplier has his cost of financing your orders priced into the merchandise. You will likely be paying a hidden interest charge, but in most cases this charge is less than what a bank or other source might want for a similar loan—and the supplier is very anxious to set up your credit if you will only supply convincing reasons of your credit worthiness.

This is the beauty of supplier credit: they are almost begging you to use their credit line while banks and other institutions may act as if you are somehow an inferior human being as you approach them for a loan. And suppliers are in your industry—they already believe it is a great business. You don't have to convince them that horticulture is a bonafide member of American industry (this is often a stumbling block at other lending agencies). Banks sometimes refuse to make horticultural loans because they don't regard such ventures as part of the mainstream business community—bankers are very conservative, and they don't like to get involved in anything they haven't seen a hundred times before.

There is another plus to supplier credit—you may often be able to extend the terms easily by simply not paying your bill on time. Although most suppliers specify that they charge interest on unpaid balances, many do not make a policy of actually trying to collect it. If your terms state net 30 days, you can often pay the bill within 60 days and the supplier will still be happy. The downside of not paying on time is that you risk alienating a good source of credit— don't employ this tactic too often, and don't do it without good reason.

There are several points to summarize again before leaving the subject of supplier credit.

- This is your best source of cheap, easy credit without restrictive conditions.
- Set up supplier credit early.
- Suppliers are anxious to do business. You are in the driver's seat if you take the time to convince them of your credit worthiness.
- The supplier believes in horticultural business already, other loan sources probably do not.
- Supplier credit is often free—in most cases you would pay the same price even if you paid cash.
- Know your supplier and salesperson personally; it is hard to deny a friend.
- Be sure to ask about extended terms.
- Suppliers vary greatly in their response to new credit accounts— shop until you find ones that are accommodative.

Leasing

Many people find that leasing vehicles, equipment, and facilities is an effective means of obtaining the things they need to run a business. Of course there are many requirements which cannot be obtained by leasing (consumable items such as inventory, labor costs, utilities, etc.). Although leasing is quite similar to borrowing, there are some important differences. Leasing costs are generally treated differently for tax purposes—the entire cost of leasing often is taken as business expense during the year the expense was incurred. In many cases, the lease may be terminated while the item still has considerable value; therefore, the person leasing is not obligated financially for the entire original cost. Standard leasing programs are available for many types of equipment (most notably for vehicles and similar mobile machines). These programs are often more convenient than applying for a conventional loan.

In recent years a few leasing companies have offered programs specifically set up for horticultural businesses. To my knowledge, these programs are intended for larger operators and will not be of much use for beginners who need only a few thousand dollars worth of equipment.

Unless you operate under particular circumstances where leasing may be advantageous, you are generally better off to borrow money at good rates and purchase the equipment outright. Only an analysis of each situation can show whether leasing or borrowing is a better deal.

Renting facilities and equipment differs from leasing mainly in the time span which the items are utilized. It is seldom an advantage to rent for long periods. Renting is helpful in some cases where you want to make certain a particular item will work well in your operation before it is actually purchased.

Venture capital and stock offerings

I mention these means of obtaining capital mainly to tell you to forget about them unless you plan an extremely large horticultural operation. Transactions of $1,000,000 are small potatoes for venture capital and stock offerings. Much larger deals are more often the rule.

Deferred labor costs

Under certain conditions, you may wish to consider obtaining labor for your operation by offering specific workers a future share in the business in place of a current weekly wage. This amounts to taking on partners and should be approached with a good deal of caution. It is not a good idea unless there are overwhelming benefits.

Credit cards

Everyone can make use of credit cards to some extent when running a business. Most of you are probably more familiar with this type of financial instrument than I am, so I will not comment at length other than to say money borrowed by using credit cards is usually much more expensive than arranging a commercial loan.

The big advantage to credit cards is the convenient and near universal availability of them. And, at present, some pretty hefty credit lines can be arranged by this means. Of course, the ease with which credit cards are obtained and used is always a danger for inexperienced or poorly disciplined people. Personally, I use credit cards only for daily incidental expenses or for travel—and I have arranged for a good line of credit through them for emergency purposes only.

Free money advertised

No doubt most of you have seen many headlines in various magazines proclaiming the availability of **Free Money** or **Free Grants** or **Immediate Loans**. While I cannot judge all these offers, I can say that the few I have checked into are no more than scams directed at people who have nothing better to do than chase rainbows. If you are serious about running a real business, forget about these free money programs and direct your efforts to more realistic work.

GET STARTED NOW

I must emphasize in conclusion that getting an early start at arranging financing for your business can make the difference between success and failure. Not only does an early start assure that the money is available when you need it but also at the lowest possible expense.

In many cases, there is no better way to become familiar with business financing than to plunge in and make a trial run with various avenues you might wish to employ. This method of learning the ropes costs only some of your time. There is no obligation on your part unless you sign legal papers (hopefully you will not do that until you are thoroughly familiar with each alternative).

Chapter 3

HOW TO GROW PLANTS, TREES, AND FLOWERS FASTER AND EASIER

Growing beautiful plants, trees, and flowers is a challenge. Growing them profitably as a business is even more difficult. That's why this chapter is so important. It outlines factors necessary for promoting vigorous plant growth. These points are then related to critical profit making suggestions.

Hopefully, this combined approach will quickly show you how to become a successful commercial horticulturist—without spending years using costly "hit or miss" methods that often end in failure. You will discover many of the professional secrets it took me years of hard work to learn. Follow these proven methods, and I guarantee you will avoid endless hours of unnecessary toil and heartache—your chances for success will be greatly increased.

These recommendations for growing ornamentals apply most directly to small and medium size commercial operations, but the majority of these points could just as well be utilized for larger businesses. The purely horticultural facts which are included could also apply to hobby or amateur situations where plants, trees, and flowers are grown under controlled circumstances.

This chapter provides a detailed outline of how to organize and operate a profitable plant growing business— but the individual technical details for each crop are not discussed. You can find this information in *The Greenhouse And Nursery Handbook*. Details concerning it and other helpful information are located at the end of this book.

GENERAL PRINCIPLES OF GROWING

Growing beautiful plants, trees, and flowers involves a large number of individual steps— all of which must be completed at the appropriate time and in a suitable manner. Fortunately the specific details concerning each crop can be located in a reference manual such as *The Greenhouse And Nursery Handbook*. Only a few basic guidelines need to be consistently kept in mind.

Anticipate difficulties

Commercial horticulture is a challenging career because the interaction between plants and their environment is extremely complex. The exact mechanisms of plant growth and development are unknown in many cases. And, although plants seem to flourish almost everywhere, the delicate balance between life and oblivion is fragile—it can be upset at any time by numerous factors.

Therefore, successful horticulturists must be trained to foresee future problems. And to plan corrective action before the actual need arises. We have already discussed how advance planning is critical to any business endeavor, but it must be stressed that this type of preparation is more essential in the horticultural field than almost any other.

I do not mean to discourage potential horticulturists by picturing this field as extraordinarily more difficult than others—but you must possess the ability to look ahead and keep an eye out for trouble. Other businesses probably have their own key requirements; in plant growing operations it is advanced planning.

Every business person must be versatile. By this I mean they should possess broad abilities and a capability to change quickly as conditions dictate. These traits are especially important to commercial horticulturists because they frequently face new situations. Living plants, trees, and flowers exist in a dynamic equilibrium with the environment. Constant change is inherent in the plant business—you must be ready to deal with it on a regular basis. The weather, for example, can switch from sunny and warm to blizzard conditions in a matter of hours.

Formalize and record crop schedules

The requirement for advanced planning is discussed above. But I like to emphasize crop scheduling as a separate activity since it is such a crucial part of successful commercial growing.

Crop scheduling is important because marketing of plants, trees, and flowers occurs predominantly within very restricted time periods. If the crop is not ready, it is often a total economic loss. Since living plants cannot be manufactured overnight (as is possible with many other types of merchandise), it is clear that the only way marketing time frames can be met is through careful advance scheduling.

Formalized records concerning crop planting and marketing are essential because only a few days can make the difference between success and failure. Are you willing to trust memory from year to year for your family livelihood? No sane person would, especially since good crop records are so easy to keep. Accurate scheduling is absolutely essential to success in commercial horticulture, and you must perform this task without fail.

Horticulture is a field which requires acute observation of many factors. In addition to the numerous points any business person needs to keep track of, professional horticulturists must keenly observe daily environmental and cultural conditions. Various plant characteristics such as color, form, size, and health are also very important to monitor on a regular basis. You cannot build a profitable business growing plants, trees, and flowers unless you develop a habit of carefully taking note of all the factors which influence your operation.

An important aspect of making observations is the means by which the information is expressed. In everyday practice most people express themselves predominantly by using words. While words are adequate in most cases, the business and technical fields often utilize numbers as a more precise means of communication. I believe you will be much more likely to succeed as a commercial horticulturist if you develop a habit of thinking in numerical terms whenever possible. This should make all your efforts more profitable, since the data input is less subject to error than when using words which may have multiple interpretations.

Numerical expression is often possible in cases where it is not customarily utilized. Much word data can be assigned numerical equivalents which are then used to perform mathematical analysis. You may be surprised how effective this technique is—but it usually takes some practice to begin thinking in this manner. A simple example of word verses numerical expression was given in Chapter 1. Don't be intimidated when "mathematical analysis" is mentioned—this simply means you will use simple arithmetic which was learned in grade school.

Seasonal demand requires rush work

This fact seems obvious enough, but I have encountered many persons in horticultural business who fail to "make hay while the sun shines." These people are usually not successful over the long haul.

In some cases, an entire season's success may hinge upon a weekend of furious selling. Although there are various strategies which can be employed to minimize such hectic activity, it will always be an important part of commercial horticulture. Developing a market plan which shifts at least a small amount of peak season sales into earlier and later periods is one way of avoiding this problem to some degree.

Crop safety is essential

Some types of horticultural crops must be defended constantly against adverse conditions, while others require only periodic protection. But there is no commercially utilized plant, tree, or flower that will grow into a marketable specimen without some form of protection during at least one stage of development. There are hundreds of potential hazards which can befall a crop—bad weather, insects, disease, poor growing conditions, pollution, and vandalism are only a few of the calamities which can occur.

Learning how to manage and accept risk is one of the most important tasks you will face as a grower. Not only must you deal with inclement weather, diseases, insects, and numerous other potential tragedies, you need to devise methods of pricing and marketing which take these many variables into account. Some people simply cannot deal mentally with the risks they inherently face. An even greater number do not effectively manage those risk factors which could be partially or totally eliminated. Basically, you deal with risk in two ways: 1) Plan ahead to eliminate or control any potential danger, and 2) Accept those problems which cannot be managed. The key to both modes of action is advance planning.

Almost every risk factor can be eliminated or controlled to an acceptable degree if you think ahead and carefully plan corrective action. Even those factors which cannot be anticipated or controlled can be dealt with by building a financial reserve fund specifically for this purpose. Such a program requires that you set prices at a level which allows a small proportion of each sale to be placed in this insurance fund. By this means, you have already prepared for occasional serious problems which may occur in the future.

In order to become successful, commercial horticulturists must develop a sixth sense concerning dangers to their crop. Not only should growers be instinctively aware of potential hazards, they must become technically proficient at providing conditions which minimize the possibility of crop damage.

Environmental management

The object of horticultural science is to modify naturally existing conditions so as to produce crops which are more suitable to the needs of man. Managing environmental factors is really the chief duty of anyone who grows domesticated plants, trees, and flowers—this is the defining characteristic of the horticultural discipline. Every grower must develop a second nature which unconsciously notices and processes information about the environmental factors which may affect plant growth and development.

Although the acts of marketing and scheduling are extremely important in commercial horticulture, the ultimate success of an operation hinges upon producing a beautiful crop which appeals to consumers. This goal can be attained only if proper growing conditions are provided. A complete listing of physical factors will be presented soon.

Blooms sell plants

People purchase ornamental plants, trees, and flowers primarily because they are beautiful. Ordinarily, the average consumer equates beauty with colorful blooms and will pay a higher price for material which is in bloom. It is true that certain horticultural plants such as most trees do not possess colorful flowers, but, in this case, the same general principal still holds true since consumers will purchase a tree which is leafed out more readily than one which is not.

The implications of this fact to commercial horticulturists are obvious. You will sell more plants, trees, and flowers if the primary attraction (be it flowers, fruit,

Blooms can be crucial in the marketing of flowering plants.

or leaves) is prominently displayed. Bedding plants in flower outsell green transplants by at least 5 to 1, and the same fact holds true when leafy trees are compared to dormant ones which have not yet produced leaves.

Multiuse crops profitable

If a garden plant has several potential uses such as in hanging baskets, patio planters, garden beds, and decorative florist pots, it has more market versatility than does a plant which can be utilized in only a single one of these situations. The majority of plants are not truly multiuse, but the ones which are warrant special consideration as potential crops.

As an example, certain large flowered Begonias can be utilized for all the specific situations mentioned above—therefore, if you have an oversupply of these Begonias in one market category, it is likely they can be sold for one of the other uses. This reduces the likelihood that some plants must be dumped.

Beauty primary

Oftentimes, in the hope of gaining a competitive advantage or of increasing profitability, growers try to cut corners on expenses. This may take the form of reducing labor or materials used in crop production—sometimes it can be accomplished without a lowering of crop quality (beauty), but in many cases the crop suffers a loss of appeal.

Growers must always be aware that they run the risk of ruining the entire image of ornamental plants, trees, and flowers by sacrificing beauty for the sake of economy. Some emphasis upon economy is certainly justified since the great majority of consumers could not afford to purchase plants which are perfect in every respect—but the compromises involving beauty and economy must be carefully weighed. Perhaps the greatest problem facing ornamental horticulture today is the lack of primary emphasis upon quality and beauty. Too many marketing outlets are more interested in volume and price.

Labor biggest expense

Tight control of labor costs must be practiced in order for horticultural businesses to be profitable. Control may be practiced by two general means: A) Keeping a lid on wage and benefit levels, and B) Making sure the workforce is effectively utilized. Each method of control should be employed judiciously to avoid antagonizing employees more than necessary. In many situations, a good amount of labor economy may be realized by improving management techniques and organizational methods—this route requires that the supervisor direct work more efficiently, but it often requires no sacrifice on the part of employees. Economy realized in this manner is generally preferable to situations where especially low wages are paid or excessive work loads are required.

Close communication between growing and marketing

Unfortunately, many growers have no interest in the marketing aspects of commercial horticulture. If this is the case, these people should grow plants, trees, and flowers only as a hobby, or they should work for someone else specifically as a grower. It is virtually impossible to run your own profitable horticultural business without devoting sufficient attention to both aspects of the operation. You must also combine the two parts carefully so that the entire business works as an efficient whole.

Propagating plants saves money

Starting plants from seed or cuttings is the touchiest and most critical part of producing a good crop. You must begin with vigorous, healthy, baby plants in order to make later steps in the crop cycle produce results. Since starting plants requires more expertise than any other step, many growers avoid this responsibility by purchasing small plants from propagation specialists. These experts don't work for peanuts! By purchasing a large proportion of starter plants you will increase expenses greatly. Avoid this pitfall by learning how to propagate plants, trees, and flowers effectively yourself. It is fun if you know what you are doing, and it saves a lot of money.

There are exceptional situations when it is more economical to buy seedlings or cuttings from a specialist— but evaluate each instance carefully to see if you couldn't do the same job for less cost at your own facility. Unless you monitor each purchase, it is easy to fall into the habit of letting someone else take care of all the more demanding tasks.

In order to become an effective propagator, you will need to study and practice these essential steps.

Trust important in horticulture

In many cases, the purchaser of plants, trees, and flowers is totally reliant upon the good faith of the seller. Only the grower who has cared for the plants knows the true state of their health or the exact variety designation which they should carry. Some purchasers may wish to know if pesticides have been used on a crop.

Everyone in horticulture relies upon previous people in the chain of trust. Growers rely upon material suppliers to provide on-time delivery of specialized products such as pesticides and fertilizers (which often must meet critical quality controls). Retail plant stores expect the grower to deliver healthy plants which are properly conditioned for the local climate. Consumers trust that the retailer is selling plants which will prosper under normal conditions. Finally, whenever a complaint is registered, everyone must trust that it is not made frivolously.

The horticulture industry simply cannot survive unless everyone concerned does their part in promoting a climate of confidence in the products. Basically, every product must carry a guarantee which is sufficient to instill trust.

THE PHYSICAL ENVIRONMENT
FOR GROWING

Many readers may be wondering when some actual plant growing recommendations will be mentioned. Have patience—I wanted initially to provide you with important background material about finance and business which many plant growing books totally ignore.

Even the following topics which relate more directly to growing plants, trees, and flowers may leave some readers feeling a need for specific information about individual crops. I offer no excuse for my method of presentation, except to say that it is intentionally meant to convey critical concepts about how to grow profitably rather than presenting minute details.

You can find the cultural details in other sources such as *The Greenhouse And Nursery Handbook*—but be prepared to spend days and weeks studying over 800 pages of technical material. What I want to provide in this present book is an easily understood (and easy to remember) outline of the basic concepts required for growing beautiful plants, trees, and flowers.

Information about the physical environment for growing plants is extremely voluminous and sometimes technical. The answer to most questions is readily available if you consult reference books. It is much more important for you as a grower to have a general understanding of how to find the right information than it is to have thousands of isolated facts rattling around in your head. Hopefully, the following points will help you develop a systematic approach towards locating and utilizing the specific information you require.

Law of limiting factors

Experienced gardeners generally have a practical understanding of this topic but may lack a thorough appreciation of exactly how it works and how significantly it affects plant growth. The law of limiting factors (as it relates to plants) was discovered in the 19th century by German botanists. Basically, it states that if one of the many physical requirements necessary to plant growth is lacking altogether or is present in insufficient supply, this one factor will limit plant growth even if all other requirements are adequately available.

The initial research for this law was carried out with the mineral or fertilizer requirements of plants and applies particularly well to this family of requirements. But it also seems to apply (although perhaps not as strictly) to other families of requirements (such as gases, i.e. carbon dioxide and oxygen) and between families of requirements. In other words, deficiencies in one fertilizer element may completely limit plant growth even if all other families of requirements (such as temperature, light, etc.) are present in suitable amounts.

In recent years, the law of limiting factors has perhaps been found to be more of a general principle rather than a rigid law but it still has a good deal of applicability. If the concept (as I have explained it here) still seems fuzzy after you have studied it several times, perhaps you can examine the details more completely in a basic college botany text at the local library. I believe the law (principle) of limiting factors is important enough that every commercial plant grower should understand its ramifications very well.

How plants grow

Having a basic scientific knowledge of how plants grow and develop is important to commercial horticulturists. This doesn't mean you must be familiar with all the physical, chemical, and biological details, but it does mean you should have a general understanding of basic plant science concepts. The previously discussed "law of limiting factors," is an example of the important principles with which it is necessary to become familiar. Examples of other concepts might be genetics (plant inheritance), water requirements, light requirements, etc.

In the most simple terms, green plants are a very complex chemical factory in which light energy from the sun is captured in a biochemical reaction (photosynthesis) and converted to stored chemical energy in the form of carbohydrate. These carbohydrates (energy) are then released as necessary to promote the growth, development, and reproduction of plants. Although the chemical pathways differ, plants and humans exist through similar processes—people take in already formed energy as food and then burn it to carry on life processes.

Most readers probably have a general understanding of the concepts just mentioned, some of you perhaps have advanced knowledge of their workings. But, before becoming a commercial plant grower, each of you should have an organized understanding of the main concepts comprising plant science. This information can be memorized in one afternoon by consulting any good high school biology text.

If you understand the fundamental ways in which plants grow, many of the details can be more easily assimilated as the need arises—and you will be able to see how each factor in plant growth fits in with others. By viewing the entire picture, the individual parts make better sense.

Many serious crop losses suffered by horticulturists over the years could easily have been avoided had the grower only been better acquainted with elementary botanical principles. The individual physical requirements of plants (as mentioned below) can be inferred through a more generalized knowledge.

Physical and chemical properties of soils

Perhaps no other factor affecting plant growth is less understood by most horticulturists than is the soil medium. Soil is such a common and unspectacular substance that it does not draw our immediate attention. I believe proper management of the soil medium, and the nutrient elements usually associated with it, is the single most pressing cultural problem which faces commercial horticulturists. This situation has arisen in large part because modern horticultural systems seldom employ ordinary field soil (several practical and technical reasons for using artificially blended soil media in place of field soil exist, but explaining them is beyond the scope of this short book). In earlier days, when field soil was commonly used for containerized ornamentals, it was not well understood—it just worked reasonably well naturally. The man-made soil systems which have been developed generally work better under modern growing techniques, but they require some basic knowledge to properly manage.

Simply by knowing that choosing the proper soil medium for plant growth is extremely important, you have taken the first critical step towards more profitable crop production. Next, you need to understand what soil options are available and how to evaluate their good and bad points. Then you must learn how to use the type of soil medium you choose. And, finally, you should carefully test the soil blend chosen before adapting it for full scale production. A good deal of the uncertainties concerning soil media can be eliminated by purchasing professionally developed mixes. But this costs a good deal of money, and you must still know enough about soils to make an intelligent choice between the numerous brands available. In a later chapter I will present detailed instructions about how to mix your own soil at minimal cost.

Naturally, the fertilizer and water factors—which I will soon mention—are intimately associated with soil and thereby add to the complexity of this general field. The areas of soil, mineral nutrition (fertilizers), and water should always be examined as an integrated whole—even though we may sometimes study them as separate entities in order to concentrate upon specific problems. If you are serious about growing plants, I urge you to study an easily understood and practical reference manual about soils, water and mineral nutrition. *The Greenhouse And Nursery Handbook* is one of the best sources of information about these subjects.

As a commercial horticulturist, you will use mountains of soil over the years—you must select the type you utilize with the utmost care. It should be economical, easily available, and effective. The soil media you choose will have far reaching effects upon plant growth and, ultimately, upon profitability,

Mineral or fertilizer nutrients

As growers have switched to using more or less chemically inert soil media, the management of soil nutrition has become a major factor in successful culture of ornamental plants. Whether you intend to purchase commercially manufactured nutrient systems or to prepare your own, a rudimentary understanding of basic nutrient needs and the methods of supplying them to plants is essential.

Many reasonably acceptable commercial fertilizer blends are available for use by growers—but these blends are usually at least double the price of purchasing the basic ingredients to mix yourself. A few hours invested in learning how to safely blend fertilizer ingredients can pay tremendous dividends—not only because thousands of dollars are saved over the years, but you also gain a more thorough knowledge of how various fertilizers affect crop growth and development.

Even if manufactured fertilizer blends are purchased, you should at least be aware of how to choose intelligently from among the many alternatives. Haphazard nutrient use is the cause of many crop failures.

Water quality and application

The important role which water plays in plant culture is obvious even to inexperienced persons. By weight, water normally comprises at least 85% of plant tissue. It is necessary as the background medium in which all the chemical processes of plants take place. Commercial horticulturists must be acutely aware of the many economic implications which may arise from such factors as water quality and chemistry, volume and availability, delivery, and cost.

Some of these factors can be studied with nothing more than careful application of common sense, while certain of them (especially water chemistry) can be

effectively evaluated only with specialized knowledge.
Since water is such a commonly used substance, we often
take it for granted in every day life. As a commercial
horticulturist, it will become necessary for you to progress
beyond this simple outlook and determine exactly how
water affects every aspect of your growing operation.

Even an abbreviated discussion of water is beyond
the scope of this book; suffice it to say that you must
carefully check out the quality and availability of water
sources before starting any horticultural business. And then
you must meticulously evaluate how water will affect the
crop programs which are planned.

I have observed many growing operations over the
years which were seriously affected by insufficient or
haphazard initial planning for water resources. This is
something which simply cannot be ignored in the beginning
stages of business because a poor water supply often cannot
be improved or developed further without great expense
and effort. Sometimes there is no practical solution to the
problem.

The application of water to plants and its availability
to them is greatly influenced by soil characteristics. And
since mineral nutrients enter the plant from soil solution
they are, to a large degree, dependent upon water quality
and water application procedures for their proper
availability. Thus, we can easily see that soils, water, and
mineral nutrition are intimately related and cannot properly
be studied independently from one another.

Light in plant growth and development

As was mentioned earlier, the defining characteristic
of green plants is their ability to capture, transfer, and store

light energy from the sun. Anything which affects or modifies this complex process is certain to have a large affect upon how plants grow—and, in turn, how profitably they can be grown.

Light energy affects plants fundamentally in two ways: 1) It determines how fast and how much the plant grows, and 2) It controls and modifies many of the developmental processes which occur in plants (such as reproduction and structural form). In some commercial horticulture applications, there is little the grower can do beyond simple spacing, shading, and placement of plants to alter either light intensity or quality—but in other situations (such as greenhouses and artificially lighted structures) the grower often has considerable control of the light available to crops.

Practicing light control on plants is often expensive and, in many cases, must be planned long in advance in order to provide proper and economical facilities.

A formal understanding of how light affects plant growth is often unnecessary to commercial horticulturists in those situations where little modification of this factor is either possible or desired. However, the knowledge one needs about this physical factor increases as more control is extended.

Temperature in plant growth and development

Although temperature (in contrast to light) is not a direct ingredient in plant metabolism, it does influence the entircty of chemical processes in plant tissue, and, through this, the actual physical appearance and integrity of the plant. Wilting and freezing are two phenomenon that are familiar to any gardener. They quickly make apparent the vast influence which temperature can have upon plant life—this should be good indication for observant growers that temperature can modify numerous additional processes and physical characteristics.

As with light, many situations do not lend themselves to serious temperature manipulation for crops. But modification of environmental temperature is very important under some conditions (in greenhouses) and can represent the major manipulative tool available to growers.

Numerous satisfactory technical means of altering crop temperature are available. There is really no practical limit to the scale of temperature modification. The grower must carefully determine how much environmental modification can be profitably practiced.

In general, the trend of modern commercial horticulture is to practice increased environmental management so that various marketing and production objectives can be more closely controlled. This statement applies to all factors but is especially true in regards to temperature.

Carbon dioxide and oxygen in plant growth and development

Perhaps no other environmental factors affecting plants are as consistently ignored as are these two gases. This is probably due to the fact that growers generally assume the quality and quantity of CO_2 and O_2 cannot be readily monitored or manipulated. Such assumptions may often hold true, but there are times when alteration of the available amounts of these gases is readily controlled. Modern instruments also make quick, easy measurement of both an economic reality.

Oxygen available to the roots of plants can be influenced greatly by soil porosity and structure. And irrigation practices also affect soil oxygen to a large degree. But many growers fail to realize that manipulation of this sort is actually influencing plant growth through oxygen enhancement or deprivation. Some greenhouse growers actively regulate the amount of CO_2 in the indoor air by several means—this practice is economical only in limited circumstances.

Although CO_2 and O_2 availability to plants is manageable in certain cases, growers often accomplish this objective as they are modifying other environmental factors—such as soil or water. Lack of specific attention to CO_2 and O_2 does not mean, however, that they are unimportant—it simply means they are normally present in sufficient quantity and quality for reasonable growth to take place.

Pest, disease, and pollution control

I believe that, other than labor and marketing problems, control of pests and diseases is the most persistent and unnerving task that I have faced in my horticultural career. Pests and diseases are such a nuisance because they are an unending source of surprise and destruction.

Crops can be ruined overnight unless growers maintain steady vigilance. And, once recognized, potential problems are not always easily solved. A good deal of technical expertise is required for truly effective management of pests and diseases. Patience and dedication are also necessary.

Fully 50% of pest and disease control problems can be prevented through good housekeeping practices in and

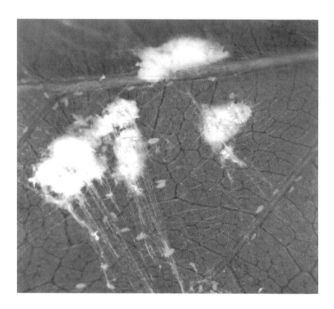

An advanced case of mealybug infestation with typical cottony web holding eggs.

around growing areas. Another 25% are avoidable by effective general business management which reduces unnecessary plant inventory and pest importation. The remaining 1/4 can be effectively managed through 1) vigilance, 2) timely response, 3) dedicated and persistent effort, and 4) technical know how.

It is easy to see that the lion's share of pest and disease control can be accomplished through rather inexpensive channels which only require common sense to apply effectively. Technical expertise is necessary only for a small proportion of control efforts.

Many growers fail to see the problems in perspective and approach it from the reverse angle. And even then they do not attack with a fully loaded gun—their level of scientific knowledge about pests and diseases is woefully limited.

More developed mealybug "crawler."

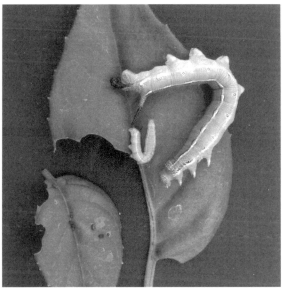

**Hornworms and the typical damage they have inflicted
upon Fuchsia leaves.**

My advice is to practice preventive common sense pest control to the fullest extent possible and only then employ technical means such as pesticides. This approach is easier, more effective and more economical.

Importance of new plant varieties

Only a few of the varieties which were grown commercially 50 years ago are in common usage today. They have been replaced for a number of reasons: 1) consumers no longer want them, 2) they have deteriorated genetically or in relation to common pests, 3) newer varieties are available which are more suitable, more economical, or more beautiful. Ash and Maple trees are a good example, numerous new varieties of these popular trees have recently been developed. They are useful for specific purposes and geographic regions.

Whatever the reason, many new varieties become available each year. This is a boon to commercial horticulturists since consumers seem to have an inborn craving for something new. Our product base in the industry is continually being revitalized so that customers do not become bored.

It is essential that every commercial grower have a systematic plan for trialing and adopting new varieties. Only a small proportion of those available will be suitable for each individual operation.

New varieties generally grow and develop somewhat differently than the ones they replace, and they will require new cultural programs. As with humans, both inheritance and culture affect the final product.

This is a good place to stress the total interrelatedness of all the physical environmental factors we have been discussing. You cannot alter one factor without affecting

Cutting or sowing Date		Open Flat	Direct Sow		Plug Flat	Crop #. Initial Pot / Later Pot Size	# Finished Fla's or Plants to Plant				Xtra Crops		Comments
Sched	Act		Plate Size	# Times to Seed			Sched	Act	+	−	Date Sown	# Flats	
11/8					406		Small						
Sow					200		Crop						
Date						1-10" Pot	25						
						2	30						
						3	30						
						4	2						
							Total:	Total:	Total:	Total:		Total:	

Comments: Dracenas, Vinca, try some with Baucopa

Variety: 10" Pot, Begonia Non-Stop

Year: 00

Schedule your crops long in advance, and then record the results carefully. This information will be the basis for future planning. A collection of reports will compose a crop "cookbook." It is a valuable part of your business.

the expression of another. This is why beautiful plants are difficult to grow—there are so many possible combinations of different physical factors and plant varieties that growing a crop is not only an exercise in technological competence but also an artistic endeavor. Only an artistically inclined person can make sense of the numerous subtle variations as they are fulfilled in the final product.

Plants need reliable and regular attention

Knowing the technical requirements for growing beautiful plants is only 1/2 of the success equation. The needs of plants must be reliably and regularly supplied in everyday practice in order that theoretical knowledge bears fruit.

Plants are silent, immobile organisms—they have no means of actively telling growers what they need, nor can they move around to secure required nourishment. This places a large burden upon the grower to determine and then supply their needs without fail. Both the grower and other employees must be extremely reliable.

Once a crop has been neglected, it is often impossible to bring it back to full potential. Extra work and care later seldom equals what was lost through early neglect.

Trial crops before commercial production

The reaction of individual varieties to specific physical environmental factors cannot be predicted with great precision. Although you may assume that related plants will perform in similar fashion—this is not always the case. And even when they do react similarly, the degree of correspondence is often not adequate for precision commercial growing purposes.

Published growing information should always be

accepted only as a general guide which can help the grower work out a specific cultural program for the exact crop. I have grown numerous Poinsettia cultivars for commercial purposes and have found that each requires a completely different cultural program. There are certainly some similarities between these Poinsettia varieties, but the differences are so pronounced that crop failure would surely result if all were given exactly the same treatment. This is why I have stressed cultural concepts in this book.

New growers do not need to reinvent the wheel each time they plan to grow a new crop, but neither should they rely too heavily upon existing cultural practices which are suitable to individual business circumstances.

Prepare for surprises

Any business that interacts with Mother Nature must be prepared for surprises. Living organisms and the factors which determine their growth and survival are so complex as to prevent perfectly predictable cultural systems from being developed. Complexity alone is not the only culprit— life itself is sometimes by nature chaotic and unpredictable.

All but the worst surprises can be handled without undue disruption if an operational plan is prepared which takes their existence into account and provides possible remedial action when and if they occur.

Make a crop cookbook

Throughout this book the general practices which are necessary to become a profitable grower of plants, trees, and flowers have been enumerated. I have refrained from giving you instructions about how to grow specific crops because there are thousands of potential crop varieties. This detail would be pointless in an introductory text.

It is up to you to choose the individual plants, trees, or flowers you wish to grow commercially. And then you should devise a crop plan for each variety by utilizing the concepts contained in this book.

When preparing crop plans you should attempt to be as systematic as possible—in other words, organize them carefully so that the various steps can be easily analyzed and followed. In this way you will be able to evaluate the results obtained each season and make minor adjustments according to your judgement. Eventually, you will wind up with a fine tuned recipe for each crop. A collection of these "recipes" will constitute a "cookbook" which is the core of your success as a commercial grower. This "cookbook" allows you to confidently and profitably grow plants year after year without worrying whether the results will be satisfactory.

STRUCTURES AND FACILITIES

I have outlined the concepts which I believe will help you become a successful commercial grower—no matter what types of plants you choose to grow. But there is one final topic that needs to be touched upon before ending.

Although some of you will grow outdoors, almost entirely without the need for production facilities, most commercial growers eventually build some type of structures. And some growers produce their crops entirely indoors in very specialized facilities. Everyone who is planning to grow plants commercially should have a basic knowledge of how to choose and utilize the structures and facilities they may need.

The generally high monetary investment required for greenhouse culture of ornamental plants requires that

Specialized indoor greenhouse facility.

growers develop an intensive management plan to fully utilize their facilities.

Many alternative greenhouse production plans are potentially profitable. Growers must select a production program which best fits their particular circumstances (which would include such factors as personal inclinations, facilities, potential markets, climate, etc.).

Under present conditions, greenhouse production schemes which emphasize growing for the recreational gardening market are likely to be the most profitable. This segment has expanded more in recent years than other markets (such as cut flowers and foliage plants) and is by far the largest in total crop value. It would seem that a grower is better to bet on a proven winner than to experiment with less proven markets.

I will summarize a few general recommendations about facilities shortly, but there is no substitute for first hand knowledge about particular options which are available. I suggest that you review these options by consulting the catalogs of manufacturers and distributors who offer them for sale. These catalogs can be easily obtained free by contacting the companies directly— instructions about how to do this along with phone numbers and addresses are contained in *The Guidebook To Wholesale Sources*.

The structures, facilities, and machines utilized to grow crops are a management tool. They help you protect crops from undesirable environmental factors, and they allow you to perform work more quickly and effectively. The only reason you should invest in such tools is if they accomplish these purposes economically. Each acquisition should be carefully evaluated beforehand on the basis of both need and economy. Structures and machines which do not add to business profits cannot be justified—they merely serve as expensive toys.

Climate important

It is vital to know the local climate before building any structure used for horticultural purposes, especially those intended for protecting crops (such as greenhouses). Records available at the U.S. Weather Service are the best source of information. Additional local weather data may be obtained from state weather services, agricultural departments, and county agents.

The usefulness of many horticultural facilities is greatly influenced by weather factors. As you evaluate weather data, pay particular attention to the extreme situations which occur rather than normal conditions. For example, you should be concerned more about maximum wind velocities, snow loads, and temperatures that your facilities must withstand than about the average days which come and go without notice. Be prepared for the worst!

Flexibility important

It is best to design structures and facilities so that they retain the maximum amount of flexibility possible while still adequately fulfilling current needs. Business requirements will change over time. If your facilities are flexible, they can be modified at a minimum of expense to meet new conditions. Before acquiring any single purpose

Cold frame tunnels used to protect shrubs from extreme cold. Note the open ends on the structures. Too much heat in winter can kill plants.

facility or machine which cannot be significantly modified or used for other purposes, you should examine the entire proposition carefully to see if there are more suitable options which allow greater latitude in choice.

Assembly line planning

Workers at a commercial nursery or greenhouse often handle thousands of plants each day. Therefore, the production facilities must be arranged in an assembly line manner to efficiently accomplish the various tasks. A good deal of planning should precede the layout of each individual assembly line area, and you must make sure they all fit together logically in the overall production process.

The assembly line in a small greenhouse or tree nursery does not usually need to be organized into a complex technological wonder such as those seen at large automobile factories—but it does need to be laid out in a logical, productive manner. And if special tools or machinery are used, they should be of a quality which allows people to work rapidly. Larger horticultural businesses may be able to efficiently utilize more sophisticated production lines.

In its most basic form, an assembly line simply means that work is arranged in a "what's next" fashion. Every step follows the previous one in a logical arrangement which allows for the most efficient and rapid movement of the product towards completion.

Production lines should be designed with a certain amount of flexibility to account for occasional glitches or necessary variations in production processes. Rigidly arranged assembly lines may be extremely efficient for single product production, but they often cannot be used for any other purpose without extensive modification.

TYPES OF ORNAMENTAL PLANTS

Classifying the thousands of ornamental plants into neat pigeon holes for convenient study is difficult. There are so many cases where a plant could as easily be placed in one category as in another, and there are numerous examples in which plants fit a particular classification under certain circumstances but more appropriately belong in another under different situations.

In spite of the difficulties, it is informative to classify plants into groups which are defined by particular parameters. The method of classification used here depends upon both the ornamental use of plants and upon major anatomical and physiologic characters. Each name given to the groups supplies readers immediate information about the entire assemblage of plants composing it.

We will be using the following classification scheme as we investigate certain topics of interest about each group.

- Bedding plants—generally meaning annuals which are planted each year to the garden and into containerized outdoor gardens.
- Herbaceous perennials—meaning those non-woody plants used in the garden which have a normal life span exceeding 2 years.
- Roses, shrubs, and trees—defined mainly by their woody character but also possessing characteristic flowers in some cases (Roses). All could also be classified as woody perennials. Many are also used as potted flowers (Roses, Azaleas, etc.), and as foliage plants (Palms, Bonsai specimens, etc.).
- Potted flowers and cut flowers—meaning those plant varieties which are commonly grown for eventual display of their flowers in the home, office, or other specific sites where decoration is desired.
- Indoor foliage plants—commonly composed of varieties having a tropical or semitropical origin which are tolerant to low light levels but also including some plants originating

from temperate climates. Certain plant groups such as Cacti, Succulents, Bonsai specimens, and water gardens are often discussed as foliage plants.

Although some commercial horticulturists grow and market a great variety of plants with different characteristics and uses, the majority tend to specialize their efforts to a greater or lesser extent. Oftentimes growers specialize in one or more of the groups mentioned above.

Specialists are certainly wise to concentrate upon learning all they can about the particular plant groups they work with, but they should also acquire some general knowledge of other ornamentals as well. This information can often be useful as business conditions evolve within the overall industry. It is not uncommon to see growers and marketers switch from one specialty area to another as circumstances change. An overall knowledge of all the different ornamentals helps business persons evaluate the most profitable crops to emphasize under particular situations.

In the presentation of plant groups which soon follows, some reference to specific varieties may occasionally be made, but we cannot begin to discuss the vast range of plant material which is available. Even a superficial study of all ornamental varieties would require many large volumes. Our purpose is to gain an overview of the subject so that you can pursue further detailed investigations.

Any person who has been active in ornamental horticulture for many years and who is familiar with at least the broad range of plant varieties now available cannot help but be amazed at the tremendous number of new and improved varieties which have eclipsed older cultivars. Horticulturists who began their career 30 years ago would find only a few varieties that were popular at that time being widely employed today. The ornamental horticulture industry is very lucky because the basic materials with which it works are extremely varied in nature and can be made almost endlessly more so through human manipulation.

Thus customers can be offered new and exciting merchandise each year. This is one important source of the public's continuing interest in plants. Commercial horticulturists who fail to realize the major role which new varieties play in drawing customers are courting disaster. Gardening and other horticulturally related pastimes have been popular in the past and will continue to prosper in the future because there is always something new. Many other industries are not so fortunate: they are dependent upon merchandise lines which may be popular for awhile, but, because of their inherently limited variability, offer little in the way of new products to stimulate continued demand.

Whatever group of plants a person works with, much attention must be placed upon discovering the new plants and the new uses which they can serve. This is a central requirement for all commercial horticulturists who hope to survive in today's extremely competitive marketplace.

Not only do horticulturists compete with one another, they are in danger of losing market share to other lines of merchandise which consumers may find attractive at the expense of plants. As long as horticulturists make sufficient effort to take advantage of the natural "newness" inherent in their merchandise, there is little chance of other products gaining in relative desirability.

Nature's variability also touches horticulturists in another way. Although much information about plants can be generalized, it will always be a field which is dominated by local experience. This is because geography and climate conspire to generate thousands of microenvironments to which plants must adjust in order to prosper. Therefore, horticulturists must always relate the information they acquire about plants to the specific climatic situations in which they will be utilized.

As you study the different groups of plants, always leave mental room for adapting this information to your local circumstances. The inability to easily find information about plants which pertains to exact situations is often a nuisance to horticulturists, but this is also one of the blessings we inherit. Commercial horticulturists who are knowledgeable about local conditions and the varieties which prosper under them are in great demand. They need have little fear that competitors will render them obsolete. Taking advantage of nature's variability to sharpen one's competitive advantage is a primary means by which commercial horticulturists can assure their continued success.

Bedding plants

Bedding plants have been the most swiftly expanding crop in ornamental horticulture during the past 2 decades. There are now indications that this growth may be slowing somewhat.

Garden plants offer both the producers and marketers a chance to move large volumes of product at profitable prices. It is a business where significant income can be generated within a short time span. And it often requires very little monetary investment.

The exciting profit potential in bedding plants is, however, realized only by a minority of growers and marketers who develop and practice effective policies which consistently provide the consumer with superior products at the opportune time. Modern shoppers are short on time and patience; they want immediate gratification of their needs now! Although price is an important concern to them, it is secondary in most consumers' minds to the service objectives mentioned above.

Although much of the explosive growth in demand for bedding plants has been fueled by chain stores featuring them as a prominent spring item, it is doubtful if this practice has resulted in booming profits for the grower supplying these markets or the garden plant department of chain stores. It has certainly caused marginally successful independent producers and marketers a good deal of trouble in the last few years.

The bedding plant industry seems to be at a watershed. Continued production and marketing with an exaggerated emphasis on low price and volume cannot continue without serious economic catastrophe for the majority of growers who supply this market segment. Although chain stores, with their great amount of merchandise diversity, may derive some eventual benefit from featuring bedding plants as loss leaders, growers generally operate a one product business and cannot survive unless they demand and receive profitable prices for their single product.

It is doubtful if the majority of larger growers have yet realized the dangerous ramifications of their headlong pursuit of volume through chain store sales. And it is even less likely that chain store garden managers realize the bottom price for bedding plants is fast approaching. Bedding plant growers simply cannot produce quality merchandise at prices appreciably below current levels. No doubt, the tug of war between producers and chain stores will eventually be concluded with results acceptable to all involved parties. But there will be some dislocations encountered before the problems are resolved—the primary pain will be felt by growers.

Wiser growers and marketers are pursuing a course of action which insulates them as much as possible from the marginally profitable segment of the industry just described. These smart operators are concentrating upon producing and marketing garden plant material which cannot effectively be handled through current chain store marketing practices. Hopefully, more growers will gravitate towards a longer range perspective which emphasizes future high profits rather than volume production at any price.

Everyone who is involved commercially with bedding plants must strive to give consumers a good product at the proper time. Accomplishing this goal requires meticulous advance planning and scheduling. The product is extremely perishable and truly popular for only a few weeks out of the year.

Production and sales records should be analyzed carefully each year in order to determine trends in consumer purchases—this is the only valid measure of what the customer wants. Too many growers and marketers handle the plants they like rather than basing decisions upon the preference of consumers.

The short season for bedding plant sales has traditionally been one of the factors which severely limits the potential for good profits. Many growers and marketers are slowly extending the marketing season to an earlier and later time frame. This is being accomplished by carefully scheduling additional product to be available at these times, and then allowing the public to vote with their purchases. In general, this has been one of the most successful marketing strategies of recent years. Anyone who does not participate in lengthening the season of use for bedding plants is bound to lose market share.

To a greater or lesser degree, the major comments we have made concerning bedding plants apply to every plant group we shall discuss. The problems and their solutions may vary somewhat, but, basically, the entire ornamental plant industry is in a transitional phase which features the traditional growers and sellers competing with low price volume oriented growers and mass marketers. Neither of these two methods of operation is inherently wrong—in fact, there are opportunities in both. But a good deal more sorting out needs to occur before the two industry segments can comfortably coexist.

The main obstacle to healthy coexistence is a lack of understanding by many participants as to exactly what role they should perform. Smaller growers and marketers must realize that they cannot compete head on with mass marketers as regards price. And smaller to medium size growers should realize that adequate profits will be hard to come by if they attempt to wholesale plants to mass marketers.

The larger growers and marketers are perhaps more realistic in their present business strategy; most of them realize that their primary objective is volume with an acceptable degree of quality. But there are some larger growers who fail to understand the problems which this strategy entails; it means razor thin profits on huge quantities of merchandise. There is little margin for error on the grower's part. In a traditionally risky business, this reliance upon small profits can prove devastating when occasional misfortunes arise.

Herbaceous perennials

The potential market for herbaceous perennial plants would seem to be quite large. Almost every consumer shopping for garden plants comments that they would like to purchase flowers which do not require being planted each year. But this theoretical demand does not always translate into actual sales.

There are several obvious reasons why total perennial demand sometimes falls short of expectations: 1) Most perennials do not bloom as continuously through the growing season as do annuals (when this is explained to consumers, they become less enthused with perennials); 2) it is often difficult to bring many perennial varieties into bloom at the opportune marketing season (impulse sales are thus reduced for perennials as compared to easily flowered annuals); 3) perennials are generally more costly to produce than similar sized annuals (therefore requiring a larger initial investment by the consumer).

Conservatively oriented growers and marketers may wish to consider the points mentioned above before they become over-enthused with some of the more optimistic demand reports for perennials. A good many of the favorable comments are undoubtedly true, but it seems that more perennials would be encountered at chain store outlets if the most optimistic scenarios are to be believed.

Even if one wished to view the perennial market with caution, there is still a good deal of potential opportunity. The very fact that this type of plant is not seen in mass market outlets in good volume would seem to indicate that more could easily be sold if they were presented properly and at the right price.

The traditional means of offering growing perennial plants has been to pot them up very early from large seedlings or from bare root transplants. This results in a big, healthy looking clump during the spring selling season—but it is an expensive method of production since propagation often occurs up to 1 year before plants are sold. Many consumers balk at the high cost of these larger plants. There has been some tendency to offer somewhat smaller plants, but seldom does one see perennials being sold as juvenile transplants in the same manner as most annuals are marketed.

It would seem that there may be a tremendous market for small perennial transplants. Many varieties can be grown on the same schedule as popular annuals, therefore making these particular perennials cost competitive. Perhaps the major reason such perennial plants are seldom encountered is simply that few growers have broken with the time worn methods of production.

Since perennials are seldom marketed in great volume by chain stores, these plants are often a high profit item for independent garden centers. Less competition means it is easier to sell at a good price.

Most temperate region perennials are quite cold tolerant; in fact, many varieties must be grown very cool to develop properly. This means that perennials may often be grown and marketed by people who lack greenhouse facilities. It is one of the least expensive methods of becoming a commercial plant grower—the main ingredients being a good deal of hard work and a small plot of land. Actual monetary outlays can be minimized by careful planning of the operation.

The thousands of perennial varieties offer individual growers and marketers alike a chance to establish themselves as experts in this field. Seldom will larger diversified growers and mass marketers feel inclined to handle any but the more popular cultivars, thus leaving a clear field for smaller entrepreneurs to exploit the large majority of perennials.

One fact which should be mentioned about perennials is their general suitability as mail order items, especially if shipped in the dormant state. Every horticulturist is familiar with the numerous magazine advertisements for perennials which occur nationwide each year. It is obviously a good business method for many people and one which every perennial grower should consider. Mail order has many benefits to offer beginning entrepreneurs, but the ins and outs of this selling method must be carefully investigated in order to assure success.

Every person who intends to grow or sell perennials locally must take into account the large number of plants sold through mail order. This competition negates, to a certain degree, the general scarcity of perennials to be found at chain store garden departments.

Various horticultural experts often campaign for garden plants to be sold in the younger stages so that they become more fully established before flowering occurs. While this may be a worthy cause, it is, in general, doomed to failure. Anyone who has observed consumers shopping for plants knows that most people are irresistibly drawn to plants which are flowering profusely. This may be the single largest stumbling block in the way of perennials becoming a truly massive crop— it is very difficult to bring most perennial varieties into bloom at the opportune marketing time. Thus the impulse buying potential of perennials is largely lost. This fact must be considered in any perennial growing or marketing plan.

Tree growers must focus on service and expertise.

Roses, shrubs and trees

The market for woody plants is perhaps even more distinctly separated into service-oriented and volume-oriented segments than are the markets for other ornamental plants. In general, most woody plants can be rather easily handled as a commodity type item by chain outlets. If reasonable efforts are made to care for woody plants, these outlets can offer the consumers a very acceptable product. Bedding plants, perennials, and flowers (as compared to woody plants) usually require more detailed and timely attention so that it is especially difficult to offer a good product under chain type marketing conditions.

The point of the previous statements is to emphasize once again that independent woody plant marketers must concentrate (even more intensely than other independent horticultural retailers) upon service and specialized products. The thousands of woody plant varieties necessary for varied geographic areas and landscape purposes offer a distinct opportunity for independent nursery owners to display their expertise. Independents may also choose to handle especially large-sized landscape plants which are inappropriate to mass marketing channels. The independent operator has many such advantages to emphasize—this is the only realistic means of competing against the price and volume strength of chains.

One aspect of woody plant production and marketing which has not received sufficient attention is the eventual survival and vigorous growth of plants in the final landscape. Most retailers and consumers assume that if a plant is adapted to the climate and looks healthy it will grow into a beautiful specimen in the landscape. This is not always the case.

Many containerized and otherwise root-restricted plants never develop properly because the root system has been injured by one or another means. The cause of injury may often be physical restriction of roots by the container or temperature extremes in the root zone. In other cases the roots have been excessively pruned prior to planting. Whatever the cause, the eventual disappointment of customers is a serious problem for the industry.

Potted and cut flowers

Flowering plants and cut flowers have traditionally been the staple crops of most year-round greenhouse growers in temperate North America. These crops were often sold at on-site retail facilities. While this scenario still persists to some extent for potted flowers, it has changed completely in the cut flower arena.

Many potted flower growers still grow for their own use or for local independent retail shops. These growers usually produce a varied line of crops and stress high quality plants for traditional flower shops. Another group of growers has now emerged which emphasizes production oriented towards mass market outlets. While these latter growers and marketers are certainly concerned with high quality, they also stress volume production and low prices. This is the old two tier marketing system we have spoken of several times.

Local cut flower production has been reduced manyfold. Fifty years ago, this was the most important greenhouse crop; now it is dominant only in a few isolated instances. In certain areas of California and Florida, cut flower crops are still big (both in the greenhouse and in outdoor fields), but a great amount of production has shifted to foreign locations such as Columbia, Israel, Spain, Australia, and The Netherlands.

The ease with which cut flowers can be shipped by jet freight has tended to concentrate their production in the most desirable and economical locations throughout the world. As a result many cut flower producers in the United States have gone out of business or shifted to other crops.

Mass market outlets have been aggressively selling potted flowers for many years, and they are now heavily into cut flowers. Therefore, we may assume that the equilibrium between independent retailers and chain stores is fairly well-established in this product area. It can easily be seen that independent flower shops are holding their own quite well, especially those which have emphasized a profitable niche which cannot be duplicated easily by chain outlets. Some independents have certainly experienced hard times or even gone out of business, but most are flourishing.

This situation shows what we may expect to happen in other areas of ornamental horticulture as the relationship between chains and independents matures. Each will hold onto that proportion of the market which it can serve best. Neither one will cause the other to become extinct.

While independent retailers have been able to hold their own, smaller growers of potted flowers have been hard hit by mass production growing methods. Many of them have been able to survive only by emphasizing spring bedding plant production more heavily.

Larger growers have turned some crops into low price commodities in many areas—Poinsettias, Mums, and Easter Lilies are examples. There are indications that this situation is easing somewhat as prices approach the lowest possible range which is profitable. Certain volume producers have been forced out of business due to insufficient profit, while others are scaling back production to more realistic figures.

Indoor foliage plants

The indoor foliage plant industry is an example of what can take place when too much emphasis is placed upon rapid expansion. In the 1970's and early 80's, foliage plant consumption increased greatly, but production increased even more quickly. Not enough attention was focused upon product quality and upon long range plans to provide a stable basis for the industry.

When consumer demand for foliage dropped slightly in the early 1980's, there resulted a severe oversupply of plants. Many growers were forced out of business and some marginal retailers curtailed their involvement with foliage plants. Only the stronger growers and marketers remained on a profitable basis.

Pothos are a popular foliage plant.

This scenario is perhaps being replayed in the bedding plant and potted flower industries today. It illustrates the folly of turning ornamental plants into a commodity rather than aiming production and marketing towards creation of a special status for these items.

Even with the shake-out which occurred in the foliage industry, there are today many growers and retailers who have adapted profitably to the new circumstances. Foliage production offers one great advantage in that it can be carried on year-round in both southern tropical locations and in northern greenhouses. But in order to prove profitable, it must be done efficiently and with careful advance planning. Quality must also be emphasized.

Even in northern greenhouses with high fuel costs, local growers who manage and market their foliage crops carefully can make money. This is not an easy task since competing southern growers can ship material north quite economically, but it can be done.

One of the main quality problems in foliage plants is the lack of acclimatization for material shipped out of southern growing regions. A good amount of these plants are not prepared properly for market. Vigorously growing plants which are shipped directly to retail outlets generally do not perform well in the indoor environment. They are not acclimated to lower indoor light levels. This situation results in less than desirable performance for consumers and a generally poor reputation for foliage plants. Such a situation inclines many people towards choosing silk or

Spider Plants are an attractive seller.

plastic plants for display.

The key to a healthy foliage plant industry is plenty of emphasis upon quality. The introduction of new varieties is also essential if the continued interest of consumers is to be expected.

PLAN EARLY FOR FUTURE PROFITS

Growing plants, trees, and flowers profitably is not an easy task which can be accomplished overnight. Hopefully, the outline of business, marketing and plant production concepts which were presented above will save a lot of time by pointing you in the proper direction to solve the many specific problems which must be dealt with as you build a successful horticultural business.

By starting now to lay the basic groundwork for a venture, you can almost guarantee that specific future projects will be accomplished easily and quickly as the need arises. There is no sense in concerning yourself with numerous details at the beginning; they will only serve as distraction from more strategic long term objectives.

Chapter 4

HOW TO CHOOSE THE BEST MONEY MAKING PLANTS

Success in the greenhouse and nursery industry results primarily from knowing how to gather and employ knowledge in an effective manner—not from working harder and harder. Many people never discover this basic fact and, as a result, either fail in business or work for only a fraction of the profits they could be enjoying.

This chapter will give you valuable knowledge about some particularly profitable ornamental plants that you might use as a "core" inventory in horticultural business. Even if you do not become a commercial horticulturist, many of the ideas presented will find application in your enjoyment of plants, trees, and flowers as a hobby or recreational activity.

First, we will discuss some of the criteria to employ when selecting various plant groups as commercial winners and then we will explore how to choose alternates for your unique circumstances. Finally, the details about specific groups of plants which are proven commercial profit centers will be listed.

PROFIT IS THE OBJECTIVE

The following points will help you develop a way of thinking which naturally leads to the selection of plant species which yield the greatest profit with the least possible effort. Many unprofitable operations I have observed over the years have no formalized criteria for judging the types of crops to grow and sell. They simply grow and sell according to their whim. This is all **wrong**!

In most businesses, a small proportion (perhaps 20%) of the merchandise line offered generates the lion's share (perhaps 80%) of the profits. A good business person quickly realizes this situation and attempts to emphasize the highly profitable items while devoting less time and effort to the least lucrative product lines.

Horticultural businesses are no different. You will generally find that a few plant varieties account for the vast majority of both sales and profits.

In fact, this general correlation between sales volume and profits for particular plant groups will soon be pointed out as one of the most significant factors you should evaluate. A good selling variety doesn't always yield high profits, but it is more likely to do so than is a slow seller.

Keep in mind that your quest is for the most profitable plants—this is the yardstick used for measure in the following discussion. A plant may be desirable in several respects, but if it isn't a good money maker—it is not considered for inclusion.

HOW TO FIND A WINNER

You may wish to develop a personal list of your own favorite money making plants or add to the one which will soon be presented. Every plant group will not be equally profitable or desirable under every circumstance. The following general suggestions will help you develop a feeling for how to begin your search.

- In most cases, highly profitable varieties are staring you straight in the face. Many of the better selling, commonly used plants are a potential gold mine (although they may presently be found in every discount store at rock bottom prices). The probable reason these varieties are so widespread is that they exhibit several good characteristics. They are unquestionably popular, and it is likely that they are easy to grow and adaptable.

  Although these popular varieties may only be marginally profitable under normal growing and marketing conditions, imaginative growers can often develop new methods which add appreciably to product appeal and value.

  One of the most significant advantages which commonly known plants possess is everyone already knows about them and recognizes that they are good varieties. All you need to do is invent new ways of reinvigorating their popularity and increasing the profit margin. Developing customer recognition and desire for plant groups is of prime importance—half this work is already completed when you work with popular varieties.

  The key means of making old varieties more profitable is to develop unusual uses, better growing methods, and more effective promotional avenues. Look over all the major plant groups you see for sale, and see if you can come up with something new. The idea may not even need to be totally new; it can simply be novel for your particular market. One unusually good brainstorm may be worth thousands of dollars if it involves an already popular variety.

- Although older more recognized varieties have been stressed as the first place you should look for highly profitable plants, you cannot neglect to seek new and unusual species which may become extremely popular if they are introduced properly. Again, these plants need not be totally new to the market; they must only seem unusual and desirable to your customers. One example I have seen recently is the use of dwarf Mugho Pine and dwarf Alberta Spruce in large containers to create miniature outdoor landscapes. Using these common shrubs and other dwarf rockery plants and flowers, you can create a truly original ready made retail item that sells for $100-$200.

Equally as important as finding new varieties is the discovery of novel trends in plant use and marketing. The product is only one part of a multifaceted growing and marketing equation.

- Expand your knowledge in order to discover anything new—be it unusual varieties, growing methods, or marketing avenues. Look around your town to see which plants are being used, and how. You will be amazed at the number of new ideas that present themselves in the course of a neighborhood stroll—that is if you are thinking about the problems at hand rather than daydreaming.

  The same exploratory procedure applies to landscape nurseries, greenhouses, horticultural sales areas, and the like. You must discover what competitors are doing and immediately copy any worthwhile ideas they come up with. After all, you are not the only one who has a brain, and it is not against the law to copy successful programs—it is simply good business tactics.

- We have already mentioned the potential profitability of older, well-recognized plant groups. Keep your eyes open for new (perhaps seemingly inconsequential) developments in these major groups. Small changes in colors, lasting or growing quality, disease resistance, etc. can sometimes herald a revolution in profitability and demand. Both Geraniums and Poinsettias have experienced tremendous market growth in recent years due to an accumulation of individual improvements.

  A small improvement to major plant groups is usually worth a great deal more than revolutionary advances with an inconsequential species.

- The remaining suggestions emphasize things you should **not** do when searching for profitable plant varieties. Never make the mistake of choosing varieties on the basis of what you personally like and dislike. Always make these choices from the standpoint of how customers actually react to specific plant species. And, whenever possible, judge the customers' response upon numerical data (however primitively measured) rather than vague guesses about how the customers appear to feel.

Some of the biggest mistakes I have made growing plants for sale commercially have resulted from letting my own preferences play too large a part in crop selection. Not everyone—not even a majority of people—will choose the same plants which appeal to you. This variety of preferences is what makes life interesting. Let customers show you what they like by allowing them to vote with their pocketbook. Your job is to tally the votes—not stuff the ballot box with meaningless personal preferences.

- A good way to find out about new plants is to read a variety of seed and other catalogs in which companies promote their new offerings of trees, vegetables, flowers, etc. But don't believe everything they say—not even a small part of it. These companies are trying to sell you merchandise, and, while most of them are reputable, they do tend to exaggerate any possible benefit when describing their products. The only way to determine if a new variety meets your standards of acceptance and profitability is to grow and sell it on a trial basis.

Never grow more than a reasonable sample the first year—no matter how enticing the descriptions sound. These plants may have performed wonderfully under the test conditions of the catalog company, but it is possible they will not react the same under your conditions. This warning, of course, applies to the crops mentioned shortly as being my favorite money makers. You should use these ideas only as a general guide to the most profitable species.

- Finally, don't pin your hopes for a highly profitable horticultural business too completely upon an unchanging merchandise line of money making plants. You must perform periodic reevaluations based upon the procedural methods you develop for crop selection. I mention this because competitors will eventually steal all your best ideas (just as I previously counseled you to do the same). You must be one step ahead of the competition by constantly selecting new money making crops. The greatest asset you can possess is not about specific money making plant varieties but how to recognize them in the first place.

PROFITABLE CHARACTERISTICS OF PLANTS

There are thousands of ornamental plant varieties in use today. Most commercial horticulturists specialize in growing and selling a small fraction of this vast array because they can manage only a relatively few species effectively. Naturally, if the selection must be limited to a reasonable number, it makes good sense to grow and sell the most profitable varieties.

As mentioned previously, the customer will ultimately tell you which species they like best—but the number offered for purchase must be prescreened to include only those plants which have a decent chance of success.

A plant group should possess specific important characteristics if it is to have any hope of being a highly profitable crop. Listed below are some of the selection criteria which are most important. You must realize that only a very few select species will possess each of these characteristics to the fullest degree—most of the better plant groups are lacking one or more vital criteria to some extent. This is where judgement and experience become important: you must be able to evaluate and balance the entire range of characteristics in order to select each species for the final test by consumer preference.

You can not expect to be correct 100% of the time in choosing potential winners. The great majority of species evaluated will be obvious losers or only worthy of minor attention. If 1 out of 10 varieties which you eventually allow consumers to test becomes truly successful, this should be considered a good batting record.

- A good species should show strong promise of being able to sell in reasonable quantity. Spend the majority of your time trying to find new uses or new marketing methods for previously established strong sellers. A plant group need not always sell in tremendous quantity to be highly profitable—it may be that it sells steadily through the year, thus making the process of growing it more predictable, more orderly, and perhaps more efficient. For example, Coleus is not an especially large crop in spring and summer, but it does sell reasonably well for shady areas outdoors. It also has a decent market in fall and winter as an indoor foliage plant.

     One thing is certain: only a tiny proportion of crops ever become profitable unless they eventually sell in reasonable quantity. If it doesn't sell very well, then the price must be high in order to recoup production costs—there is not much demand for extremely expensive plants.

- A highly profitable crop should be easy to grow for the producer and for the eventual consumer. In many cases, it also helps if the plant grows quickly. Some specific things you should look for are: A) Is it relatively pest free? B) Does it grow predictably from year to year? C) Does it grow well within a tolerable range of environmental conditions? D) Does it grow within bounds (doesn't require excessive production space)? E) Are the crop conditions it requires economical (no excessive heat source required, no excessive labor needed, etc.)? F) Does the specific crop culture it requires fit within your operational capacities? G) Is it a good keeper (remains in sellable condition over a reasonable period of time)?

     Do not neglect the need for plants to consistently perform well for customers from year to year. In my commercial operation I have encountered some species which were extremely popular and profitable for 1 or 2 years but eventually failed to be a high profit crop simply because they did not grow well for customers over an extended time frame (Martha Washington Geraniums for example).

- The most profitable crops are generally those which you can propagate reliably at your own greenhouse or nursery. If you can start the majority of your own plants, this eliminates a major cost of purchasing and transporting starter material. It also allows you to have more control over a critical phase of crop culture and to prevent the importation of exotic bugs and diseases into the production area.

- Plants that can be used for several different purposes are often more profitable to grow and sell than are those with a single limited application. For instance—Petunias or Impatiens have a variety of uses in flower beds, porch planters, and hanging baskets; thus they are a bigger money making crop than perennial Primroses which are not so versatile.

    Multipurpose plants not only sell better, they sometimes offer the producer a chance to move inventory between different product uses, depending upon which one is in demand at that particular time.

- Plants which are not widely available elsewhere in sufficient quality or quantity are often a good bet for high profits. Geraniums and Rose plants are a case in point—while both are widely promoted at cheap prices by discount stores, these items are seldom of the quality which discerning gardeners prefer. Therefore, high quality and larger specimens of Roses and Geraniums are often very profitable for the independent grower who caters to the dedicated gardener.

    Even when very popular varieties are widely available in good quality at discount stores, there is every chance that you can make good money offering similar merchandise simply by having plenty of stock available at all times. During peak seasons, the chain stores may not have sufficient merchandise available to meet demand, and many customers will then purchase your plants even if the price is considerably higher.

- It must be stressed again that plant varieties which are highly profitable in the long run must perform well for the customer. You want to concentrate upon plant groups which reliably make money year after year, not those which do well for a season or two and then fail because consumers find the plants don't measure up to initial expectations.

MODIFYING FACTORS APPLYING TO PLANT LIST

During the past 25 years, the use of garden plants has grown tremendously. This is where the big profits have been in ornamental horticulture, and it is the main reason the following list of plant varieties focuses primarily upon garden plants. I have many plants that I like to grow and sell but most of them do not make a good deal of money simply because they do not sell in the same large volume as do spring garden plants.

Also, you will notice that, even though most of them can be grown without protection, few woody plants are listed. The culture of woody plants is somewhat more specialized; I thought it best to generally restrict discussion to those varieties which are better suited to small scale local production and to those in which on premises propagation is more easily possible.

These plant groups reflect my personal experiences. You must interpret the results based upon the fact that I am a medium size local grower who specializes in selling to a rather upscale market. My production is highly labor intensive and aimed towards consumers that demand high quality. Large growers who specialize in the wholesale trade for mass markets may find that my list is partially unsuitable for their purposes.

Growers who live in extreme climates such as the Desert Southwest or a temperate rain forest may need to evaluate these recommendations for light and temperature somewhat differently than persons who live in more moderate climates. Full sun means something different to a person living in Michigan as opposed to a resident of Arizona. The temperature and light ranges given represent, as much as possible, a middle ground.

Growth of the plant varieties mentioned is generally good under a wide variety of circumstances. This is perhaps one reason why many of them are listed. But you must understand that some, such as Impatiens and Petunias, grow best at opposite extremes of environmental conditions. Impatiens are popular in the shady east, while Petunias are more widely grown in the western sun belt.

All these plants may be assumed to grow well under normal cultural conditions of fertilizer, water, and soil unless specific mention of exceptional needs is made in the special comments section which follows each variety.

BEST MONEY MAKING PLANTS

Deciding which plant varieties to include in this list has not been an easy task. There are many more I would like to emphasize, but our immediate task is to pick the top performers.

Do not accept this list uncritically, you may wish to add or delete species based upon your own judgement. Use the various criteria mentioned previously to help make your choices. *The Greenhouse and Nursery Handbook* is a good source of information for other useful species and for many cultural details (which I have necessarily omitted from this small book).

Although an attempt to mention some climatic and geographical variations will be made as the plant groups are discussed, please remain alert to interpret all the information in relation to the particular circumstances which exist in your locale. Persons who live in extreme southern or coastal regions should take heed of this advice more carefully since the descriptions presented apply most closely to the interior of North America.

The temperatures mentioned refer to night unless

otherwise noted. Day temperatures may generally be allowed to increase 10-25° F from night time. Varieties are listed alphabetically, and no importance should be attached to their order of appearance.

Established growers should evaluate the following list to make certain each of the plants mentioned is in their program. If one or more is missing, there should be a good reason for the omission; each one is a proven money maker.

New growers need to consider each of these plant groups which makes sense under their proposed business plans. All of these plants may not fit into your cultural methods, but I think many of them will. Hopefully, by using this information, you can quickly establish a core group of profitable crops. This is something that took me years of trial and error to accomplish.

Readers who are unfamiliar with one or more plants mentioned can easily consult *The Greenhouse and Nursery Handbook* or *The Illustrated Handbook of Landscape Plants.* In addition to more complete descriptions of the various species, photographs are presented.

Alyssum

- **Principal uses:** Annual flower gardens and mixed combination pots where a low growing plant is needed.
- **Sales potential and season:** A great seller in spring and early summer. Blooms profusely and smells heavenly. Quick growth and inexpensive seed make Alyssum very profitable.
- **Propagation methods:** By seed which is generally very inexpensive. Multiple seedlings may be transplanted to small pots or several seeds can be broadcast in the final container since germination is extremely vigorous.
- **Growth in greenhouse or nursery:** Very vigorous, blooms in as little as 6 weeks from seed but must receive careful attention in early stages to produce a uniform crop.
- **Pests and diseases:** Insects are usually no problem, but

various fungal diseases can devastate seedlings. Provide plenty of fresh air and do not over water.
- **Temperature preference:** Germinate at 65-70° F, and then grow early stages at 55-60° F until well-established. Better plants result when the temperature is dropped to 45-50° F during the last 1/2 of the crop schedule.
- **Light preference:** Full sun. Plants quickly become leggy and blooming is inhibited when shaded.
- **Special comments:** The key to selling lots of annual Alyssum is to schedule crops so that new material is ready as needed. Although freshly blooming Alyssum is almost irresistible, old plants quickly become unsalable. White flowered varieties generally bloom earlier than do pink and purple. White is also more fragrant. Specific seed selections vary greatly in performance; try several until you get one that does well for you.

Asparagus Sprengeri

- **Principal uses:** Greenery in spring and summer, annual flower pots, and hanging baskets. Also used as an inexpensive foliage plant in high light indoor situations and as filler and greenery in cut flower arrangements.
- **Sales potential and season:** Although Sprengeri sells only in limited quantities, it does have year around uses so that it can be profitably grown in every month of the year.
- **Propagation methods:** By seed. Germination is slow and irregular over a period of 25-45 days after planting at 75° F. Seed must be a fresh crop since it soon loses viability.
- **Growth in greenhouse or nursery:** Does not grow as fast as some annuals, but it is a quick grower when compared to other indoor foliage plants. Very easy culture.
- **Pests and diseases:** Aphids love the tender new shoot tips. No major disease problems.
- **Temperature preference:** Grow at 55-65° F for the most compact plants. If you want looser, more hanging foliage then grow at 65-70° F.
- **Light preference:** Full sun in areas where outdoor sunlight is less intense or semi-shade in high light climates. Generally full sun if indoors. Will grow in fairly shaded situations but

plants become rangier.
- **Special comments:** Asparagus Sprengeri is one of the most useful multipurpose ornamental plants. It grows easily at all seasons but must be planned long in advance since a heavy 4 inch pot takes from 6-12 months to produce from seed (depending on temperature and planting date). Mature plants must not be allowed to dry out since the needle-like leaves yellow up and drop off easily if plants are subjected to drought. Best to grow on the moist side when fully developed.

Bacopa

- **Principal uses:** Annual garden flower, very useful as a trailing filler in combination pots and hanging baskets.
- **Sales potential and season:** Produces masses of small delicate flowers from early spring to late fall. The best display is during cooler weather or in slight shade during summer.
- **Propagation methods:** From cuttings, roots easily if cuttings are clean and not allowed to wilt during first 4 or 5 days. Remove from mist after this time to prevent rot which quickly develops in wet situations.
- **Growth in greenhouse or nursery:** Easily grown if day temperatures can be held under 85° F. Slight shade recommended in summer. Pinch to develop good branching. Crowded plants and poor ventilation encourage stem and leaf rot.
- **Pests and diseases:** Most common pests attack Bacopa, but mealybug and white fly are the primary offenders if control efforts are poor. Plants develop thick growth over time which can lead to stem and leaf rot.
- **Temperature preference:** Best production if grown cool from 50-60° F when established but tolerates higher and lower temperatures quite well unless subjected to extremes every day.
- **Light preference:** Full sun except in high light areas where moderate shade may be required during midsummer.
- **Special comments:** One of the best selling and most useful plants to come along in years. Seldom seen 10 years ago. White Bacopa is most popular because it produces a snowy cascade of flowers on semi-trailing plants, hence the common name of "Snowdrift" or "Montana White". Blue or lavender forms such as "Mauve Mist" or "Blue Mist" are very

floriferous and decidedly more trailing in habit but don't seem to tolerate summer heat so well.

Cacti and Succulents

- **Principal uses:** Indoor plants for high light areas. Outdoor patio planters in summer or year-round in mild climates. Rock garden displays.
- **Sales potential and season:** Reasonable sales year-round for indoor uses. Certain climatic areas may have considerable demand for outdoor plants.
- **Propagation methods:** Seed, cuttings, divisions. Exact methods and conditions necessary may vary but generally do best when humidity and moisture are minimal.
- **Growth in greenhouse or nursery:** Cacti and harder leaved

Cacti and succulents can be combined in pots for creative marketing.

Succulents may be very slow. Many softer Succulents and some Cacti grow fairly quickly. A few Succulents exhibit rapid growth. Need reduced moisture and fertilizer.

- **Pests and diseases:** Most pests become a problem only if prevention is ignored. Diseases are seldom serious unless excess moisture is available.
- **Temperature preference:** Best growing temperature is 60-75° F for most species, but lower temperatures generally are tolerated and sometimes even beneficial. Contrary to popular thought, higher temperatures seldom promote better or faster growth.
- **Light preference:** Full sun. Many species may tolerate light shade without noticeable ill effects. Almost none prefer shade.
- **Special comments:** This is a big group of plants. You can select a limited number of those species which grow and reproduce easily. They can be sold individually or as combination pots. The slower growing varieties are seldom a big profit center for smaller growers—generally, they are grown by specialists who operate in warmer climates. A low labor crop which thrives on neglect if proper basic conditions are provided.

Chrysanthemum

- **Principal uses:** Perennial garden flower. A leading potted and cut flower.
- **Sales potential and season:** The number 1 fall blooming perennial. Can be sold in bloom in spring or fall. Good demand in the floral trade.
- **Propagation methods:** Mainly from cuttings offered by specialist propagators. A few seed varieties. Usually best to obtain disease free cuttings rather than propagate your own.
- **Growth in greenhouse or nursery:** Grows quickly and vigorously, but good attention must be paid to pest and disease control, critical temperatures and day length. Heavy feeder.
- **Pests and disease:** Diseases are seldom a problem if you purchase cuttings from reliable propagators. Aphids are the main pest, other insects can also become established if preventive control is not practiced.
- **Temperature preference:** Safest to maintain temperatures

above 60° F for bud set; garden varieties will generally set bud at temperatures down to 50° or 55° F. Excessive night or day temperatures can delay or prevent bud set.

- **Light preference:** Full sun. Chrysanthemums are an extremely day length sensitive crop. Variations in this factor are the main consideration when timing the bloom period.
- **Special comments:** Smaller growers generally will be best off to focus on the garden plant market. Flowering pots and cut flowers are relatively easy to grow if attention is paid to details but numerous large growers have flooded the market with product on a year-round basis. Garden Mums are easy to produce and sell in good quantity—one of the best profit makers.

Garden Mums are a perennial profit maker.

Coleus

- **Principal uses:** Brilliantly colored foliage accent plant outdoors in spring and summer. Inexpensive indoor foliage plant.
- **Sales potential and season:** A good selling outdoor plant in climates with less intense sun, moderate spring bedding sales even in sunny areas. Year-round steady sales as indoor foliage.
- **Propagation methods:** Both seeds and cuttings start easily. Seeds more common for mass garden sales. Start both at 75° F.
- **Growth in greenhouse and nursery:** Rapid and easy when in vegetative phase. Winter flowering occurs in northern greenhouses and limits growth unless day length is extended by artificial lighting.
- **Pests and diseases:** Insect pests not serious unless allowed to establish without control measures. Various stem and root rots can be serious if over watering occurs. Plenty of ventilation and warm temperatures help avoid disease.
- **Temperature preference:** Warm, 65-70° F is ideal, but plants will grow reasonably well 10° F either side of this range.
- **Light preference:** Shade outdoors in all climates except those where sun intensity is low. Good sun indoors. Some new varieties are available which are touted as full sun plants in all but the sunniest climates.
- **Special comments:** Coleus is not one of the very best selling bedding plants, but it has many other uses through the year. The steady nature of sales year-round and easy culture make Coleus a real money maker. It makes impressive patio planters and hanging baskets which can be sold at high prices. Many exciting leaf colors are available—well done large plants are very eye catching.

Cucumber and Squash

- **Principal uses:** Spring vegetable gardens.
- **Sales potential and season:** Both sell extremely well for a limited period of time.
- **Propagation methods:** Seed. Germinate 3 seeds directly in each selling container. They sprout quickly at 55-80° F.

- **Growth in greenhouse or nursery:** Very fast, can be sold in 3-4 inch pots within 3-4 weeks of sowing. Squash is especially fast. Watermelons and Cantaloupe react similarly but must have higher average temperatures.
- **Pests and diseases:** No serious disease or insect pests if normal precautions taken. Mice can ruin an entire crop overnight by digging up and eating seed. Trap every mouse before planting. Warn customers not to separate seedlings; plants do not transplant easily—they must be handled carefully. Plants will not tolerate cold temperatures.
- **Temperature preference:** Grow at 50-65° F after germination. Can tolerate higher temperatures but growth is leggy and weak.
- **Light preference:** Full sun.
- **Special comments:** This is without doubt the highest profit crop of all, and it sells well. Only the limited sales time is a drawback. Choose your varieties carefully, as some do not set fruit unless more than one plant or more than one variety is present. Planting 3 seeds per pot solves the problem of needing multiple plants for fruit set, and it makes a nice plant faster. Since plants grow quickly and the marketing window is short, scheduling must be done carefully to assure plenty of high quality product at the proper time.

Cyclamen

- **Principal uses:** A major flowering pot plant during cooler months.
- **Sales potential and season:** Many growers should emphasize this low labor crop more. Can be the major winter and early spring flower crop if promoted. Southern greenhouses can do well with Cyclamen in winter.
- **Propagation methods:** Seed. Germinate at 60-70° F. Best varieties must be sown 6-9 months before flowering and grown shady during summer. Southern growers will probably wish to purchase small plants for late fall planting.
- **Growth in greenhouse or nursery:** An easily grown crop if basic environmental factors are maintained. Rather slow—this is why there is often a shortage of good Cyclamen.
- **Pests and diseases:** Spider mites can become serious if early

precautions are not taken. Crown rot is often a problem if temperatures are too low and moisture is high. Provide good air circulation.
- **Temperature preference:** Will tolerate very low temperatures but growth is retarded. Commercial production for faster crops requires 55-60° F. This higher temperature also reduces incidence of crown rot. Cyclamen do not like excessive summer heat and extreme sun; you must be sure that shady, cool conditions are provided at this time.
- **Light preference:** Full sun late fall through early spring in north. Shade in warmer months. Southern growers may need to shade lightly in winter.
- **Special comments:** The Cyclamen is a very popular winter flower that can be easily produced by most every smaller grower if they have the patience for long crop cycles. Not as yet overdone in discount stores. The bulbs which develop on seedlings should not be buried, as this leads to crown rot. Place only the bottom portion of the bulb in soil.

Dianthus
- **Principal uses:** A large group of perennial and hardy annual garden plants. Some species (especially Carnations) are also useful as potted and cut flowers.
- **Sales potential and season:** Spring, early summer sales are very good in most climates. In mild climates, you can sell many garden Dianthus for winter annuals.
- **Propagation methods:** Seed in most cases. Divisions and cuttings are common for certain groups. Cuttings are the primary means of reproduction for Carnation cut flowers.
- **Growth in greenhouse or nursery:** The entire Dianthus group grows easily but requires lower temperatures and fertilizer in order to avoid lush growth. Over watering can also cause the same problem.
- **Pests and diseases:** Aphids are the main pest and can become serious if preventive measures are not taken. Diseases are not generally a problem if reasonable attention is paid to cleanliness and cultural factors.
- **Temperature preference:** Dianthus like it cool. Most do best at 40-55° F after establishment at higher temperatures. Will

generally tolerate light frost, and, when acclimated, they will survive heavy frost.

- **Light preference:** Full sun. Shady conditions cause tall, spindly plants.
- **Special comments:** Dianthus contains many useful garden varieties for the small grower. Not often a big item at chain stores because good stocky plants are not easily grown without careful attention to detail. Hardy annual types are especially colorful and have proven to exhibit good perennial characteristics even in my harsh winter climate.

Dusty Miller

- **Principal uses:** Silvery foliage accent plant for spring and fall gardens, patio planters, and hanging baskets. Occasionally used as foliage in cut flower arrangements.

Dusty Miller makes an attractive accent plant.

- **Sales potential and season:** Has exceptional sales possibilities if it is shown in potential uses. Since it does not flower extravagantly its usefulness must be demonstrated. Plants are extremely cold hardy and will exhibit nice silver foliage outdoors until Christmas in all but the harshest winter climates.
- **Propagation methods:** Can be taken as cuttings but almost always propagated by seed. Germinate at 65-80° F, establish well at 55-65° F, and then drop temperature to 45-60° F during last half of growing period.
- **Growth in greenhouse or nursery:** Easy to grow, but seedlings must be established carefully. Crowded or overly wet plants will develop leaf and stem rot easily.
- **Pests and diseases:** Aphids can become troublesome if control is neglected. Disease problems minimal except as noted above.
- **Temperature preference:** Likes warm temperatures to start but can be grown well in later stages even with occasional light frost at night. Heavy frost is tolerated in the garden if acclimated gradually.
- **Light preference:** Full sun. Can be used in slightly shaded garden situations or in shade type hanging baskets and planters, but growth is not as compact and as intensely silver as in full sun.
- **Special comments:** Dusty Miller is a garden plant which could reach major crop status if its exceptional garden performance was promoted to the fullest extent. Could be used as a winter annual in moderate climates. Since it is easy to grow, and keeps well on display, it is very profitable.

Geranium

- **Principal uses:** Garden beds, patio planters, and outdoor hanging baskets. A good indoor bloomer for sunny spots. Large pots are a perfect gift for Mother's Day.
- **Sales potential and season:** One of the most popular spring and summer flowers. A great seller if you offer modern varieties in a broad choice of colors.
- **Propagation methods:** Seed propagation is popular for inexpensive plants, but vegetative cuttings are still preferred

for the most desirable plants.

- **Growth in greenhouse or nursery:** Easy to grow nice plants quickly if attention is paid to cultural details. Don't forget to produce a good number of larger pots for demanding customers.
- **Pests and diseases:** No serious pests if preventive measures are taken. Diseases are no problem if certified disease free stock is used for planting or mother plants. Do not attempt to hold mother plants from year to year.
- **Temperature preference:** Propagation and establishment 70-80° F. Finish the crop at 55-65° F. Higher and lower temperatures can be tolerated, but crop quality deteriorates.
- **Light preference:** Full sun. Some shade is tolerated in extremely high light areas.
- **Special comments:** Geraniums sell in volume, but strong competition means you must pay attention to every detail in order to produce good quality plants that sell profitably. Seed Geraniums are easier to grow but do not generally produce the exceptional blooms that discriminating buyers prefer. Don't forget Ivy Geraniums, as they are important for hanging baskets and planters. Modern disease free stock is absolutely necessary for profitable production.

Grape Ivy

- **Principal uses:** A trailing indoor foliage plant for relatively low light areas. Easily trained to a trellis for specimens or as a room divider.
- **Sales potential and season:** Good demand all year as an indoor plant. Can be used as a shady trailer outdoors in summer or in mild winter climates.
- **Propagation methods:** From cuttings generally, but seed is sometimes available.
- **Growth in greenhouse or nursery:** Plants are slow to start but grow more easily once established. Needs a light, well-drained and highly organic soil.
- **Pests and diseases:** Mealybugs can be troublesome unless controlled. Grape Ivy is very susceptible to mildew unless ideal atmospheric and temperature controls are practiced. Easiest way to avoid mildew is to spray all plants periodically

Blooming geraniums are difficult for customers to resist.

with a suitable fungicide.

- **Temperature preference:** Best specimens are produced at 60-70° F in greenhouses. This is one reason large crops for export are usually not produced in Florida, thereby making Grape Ivy in short supply compared to other foliage varieties. A good item for local northern greenhouses.
- **Light preference:** Light shade in winter greenhouses, heavy shade in summer. Moderate to lower light in interior landscape. This is one of the easier plants to care for indoors. Maintains a lustrous, dark green leaf color.
- **Special comments:** Since it is easy to grow, long-lived, and tolerates rather low light, Grape Ivy is one of the premier indoor plants. Coupled with the relatively short supply it makes a good profit item. Mildew control is the main problem for growers, but, if plants are disease free when sold, they rarely develop this disease in the home or office. Two common varieties— regular pointed leaf and oak leaf with rounded leaf tips.

Hibiscus

- **Principal uses:** Potted flowers. Outdoor flowering shrubs.
- **Sales potential and season:** Sells steadily all year as a potted flower and interior landscape plant for sunny areas. A popular shrub for tropical and subtropical outdoor landscapes. Some varieties are suitable for landscaping in colder climates.
- **Propagation methods:** Usually by cuttings. Root under mist at 70-80° F.
- **Growth in greenhouse or nursery:** Grows easily and quickly. Must be watered and fertilized adequately without large excesses. Usually needs extra iron to develop a good green color in the leaves. Blooms at any season.
- **Pests and diseases:** Aphids and spider mites become easily established. White flies are serious if plants are exposed to infection. No serious diseases.
- **Temperature preference:** Best temperature in the greenhouse is 70°F, but plants will tolerate higher and lower. Cold climate landscaping varieties can be grown cooler.
- **Light preference:** Full sun. When plants are ready to flower, they can be placed in slightly shaded locations and continue to bloom well.
- **Special comments:** Hibiscus have become one of the most popular flowering plants in recent years. The flowers are exceptionally beautiful. They can be grown through the summer and fall in northern greenhouses. Winter production is difficult unless plenty of sun and good heat are available. Hibiscus make nice patio planters in summer. Cold hardy varieties should be used more in northern landscapes.

Impatiens

- **Principal uses:** Outdoor garden beds, patio planters, hanging baskets. Nice indoor blooming plant for sunny spots in winter. New Guinea Impatiens make an inexpensive flowering pot for gifts.
- **Sales potential and season:** Impatiens is the largest selling garden plant in America. Not as popular in high light areas but still important. Small but steady sales through winter as a blooming window plant.

- **Propagation methods:** Seed or cuttings. Inexpensive garden plants mostly by seed which is touchy to germinate properly. New Guinea Impatiens primarily by cuttings but limited seed varieties are available.
- **Growth in greenhouse or nursery:** Easy, quick growth if warm temperatures are provided. Plants will not tolerate high salt water. Fertilizer must be limited or growth becomes overly lush and weak.
- **Pests and diseases:** Most pests can become established unless decent control measures are employed. Spider mites are the most frequent problem. Mealybugs are common on New Guinea Impatiens. Stem and root rot are likely if temperatures are cool and over watering occurs. Damping off is common on seedlings
- **Temperature preference:** Germinate at 65-80° F. Grow young plants at 60-70° F. Lower and higher temperatures can be tolerated but quality of growth is impaired.
- **Light preference:** Impatiens do not tolerate extremely sunny locations, but some varieties are being introduced which perform well in all but the sunniest climates.
- **Special comments:** There is lots of competition in the Impatiens market but also much opportunity for volume sales. The key to success is attention to every detail of crop culture and production of high end specialty items such as porch planters and hanging baskets. Pay attention to selecting only the very best varieties. Since seed germination is sometimes difficult, you may wish to consider purchasing established seedling plugs from specialist growers or resort to purchasing "enhanced" seed.

Ivy

- **Principal uses:** Indoor foliage plant for high light areas. Outdoor perennial ground cover and climber. Useful as trailing filler in cut flower arrangements and bridal bouquets.
- **Sales potential and season:** The market for Ivy is not spectacular, but it continues to be steady in most all seasons. Good customer recognition.
- **Propagation methods:** Cuttings. Easily rooted at 60-80° F. Many varieties are available. Discussion here refers mainly to

the English or California types of true Ivy (Hedra), but there is considerable outdoor use of other plants which are erroneously called Ivy (Boston Ivy, Virginia Creeper, etc.).

- **Growth in greenhouse or nursery:** Very easy and relatively fast at 60-70° F. One of the most foolproof inexpensive foliage plants available.
- **Pests and diseases:** Spider mites can be very serious unless precautions are taken to avoid exposure. No serious diseases under reasonably sanitary culture.
- **Temperature preference:** Tolerates a wide variety of temperature and still produces acceptable plants.
- **Light preference:** High light indoors for best growth but will tolerate some shade. Prefers some shade outdoors if the sun is intense.
- **Special comments:** Steady year-round sales, easy culture, and a variety of uses combine to make Ivy a very profitable item for anyone who grows plants throughout the year.

Lilacs

- **Principal uses:** Flowering landscape shrub, sometimes used as hedges or small trees.
- **Sales potential and season:** Can be sold containerized from late winter through fall. Mostly in areas with pronounced cold winters. The majority of sales occur when Lilacs bloom naturally in the local landscape. Everyone in Canada and the northern United States is familiar with Lilacs so there is a steady demand.
- **Propagation methods:** Seed for some varieties (especially common Lilacs), suckers, cuttings. Suckers of common purple and white Lilacs are the easiest method for small retail growers or purchase inexpensive seedlings from specialists. For other varieties purchase bare root plants wholesale.
- **Growth in greenhouse or nursery:** Best to pot multiple seedlings or small suckers in 1 or 2 gallon pots in early spring or late fall. Leave outdoors and mulch the pots for winter protection. Sell the next spring. New spring transplants make very little leaf and stem growth the first growing season, but fall transplants that root in during winter leaf out well the following spring.

- **Pests and diseases:** Scale is a common pest unless precautions are taken.
- **Temperature preference:** Normal outdoor temperatures in northern latitudes. Keep pots mulched in winter to prevent alternate freezing and thawing damage. Better growth usually results when pots are protected from heat build up in summer if grown in high light areas.
- **Light preference:** Some shade after transplanting may be beneficial, but full sun is okay after rooted.
- **Special comments:** Lilacs are not a grower's dream. However, due to the fact that there is steady demand for these popular shrubs and because plants that have not been over wintered in the pots usually look unacceptable for discriminating buyers, growers who wish to pot up before winter sets in can command premium prices. Common Lilacs are the least expensive varieties to deal with, but numerous hybrid selections are available. Smaller plants of hybrids are usually hard to find. The Korean Lilac is a dwarf variety which blooms well the first spring after transplanting from rather small stock—most varieties do not. Lilac tree selections are also available. There is little advantage to potting Lilacs during spring since fall planting seems to yield approximately the same results without the need to care for potted stock the first summer.

Lipstick Plant

- **Principal uses:** Indoor blooming foliage plant. Principally used in hanging baskets or smaller pots.
- **Sales potential and season:** Sells steady all year as indoor plant. Much better market when plants are blooming freely.
- **Propagation methods:** Usually by cuttings. Seed may be used in some cases. Grow in a well-drained, highly organic soil.
- **Growth in greenhouse or nursery:** Easy grower, but better blooming varieties are rather slow to produce a quality basket. Some varieties which don't have conspicuous blooms produce vigorous attractive foliage and are best used for vegetative characteristics rather than flowers.
- **Pests and diseases:** Not particularly susceptible to most common pests. Problems can arise if control procedures are inadequate.

- **Temperature preference:** Tolerates a wide range of temperature but does best at 65-75° F.
- **Light preference:** Enjoys good light but will not tolerate full sun in the greenhouse. Leaves burn easily in summer if light intensity is too high.
- **Special comments:** Lipstick Plant is one of the more durable indoor plants that flower well. Most retail foliage customers ask two questions: 1) Is it easy to grow? 2) Does it flower? This is one of the few plants that fills both qualifications. Even though Lipstick is relatively unknown to most people, the bright scarlet "lipstick" tubes emerging from a burgundy-colored base draw attention instantly.

  Large commercial growers seldom offer Lipsticks— probably because they are a long term crop that is relatively hard to get started well. The plants, however, grow easily once they are larger. Being a rather expensive plant to produce means that few mass merchants are interested in them. This leaves the local grower who caters to upscale customers free to set a profitable price on these gorgeous plants.

  Lipsticks usually bloom well about twice a year on older wood—most commonly in spring and fall. The blooms last for a good while. Plants should be pruned well several months in advance of anticipated bloom to develop numerous bud sites.

Marigold

- **Principal uses:** Outdoor garden beds, patio planters, combination hanging baskets. Occasionally as an inexpensive cut flower.
- **Sales potential and season:** Basically a spring and summer bedding plant. One of the more popular groups of plants in sunnier regions. Less popular in shady climates.
- **Propagation methods:** Seed. Germinates quickly and easily at 55-70° F. Some of the newer varieties are expensive but well worth the extra cost if chosen carefully.
- **Growth in greenhouse or nursery:** Very fast and easy if warm temperatures (55-65° F) are provided to start and adequate fertilizer is applied. Last 1/2 of crop cycles can be 45-60° F.

Marigolds in bloom are always popular.

- **Pests and diseases:** Despite popular tales to the contrary, aphids love Marigolds and will ruin crops unless guarded against. Over watering leads to stem and leaf rot on crowded plants.
- **Temperature preference:** Marigolds will tolerate a wide range of temperatures but grow best at the medium range of 50-60° F. Very susceptible to frost damage.
- **Light preference:** Full sun. Some varieties are responsive to photoperiod for flowering. Check seed books to determine what day lengths promote best flowering.
- **Special comments:** Marigolds are a grower's dream plant if details are followed and fertilization is adequate. Many size groups are available for different garden needs. Color selection is a major drawback—available generally only in yellow, orange, and maroon variations. Mice love the seed so make sure a trapping program is conducted prior to sowing seed.

Pansy

- **Principal uses:** Flower beds. Use in hanging baskets and patio planters is increasing, especially for cool weather months.
- **Sales potential and season:** Extremely popular in early spring and less so in cool fall months. As a winter annual in mild climates.
- **Propagation methods:** Seed. Germinates best at 55-65° F. Most seed is extremely expensive. Mice love it and can destroy an entire sowing in a few hours.
- **Growth in greenhouse or nursery:** Easy and quick to flower. Over fertilization and overwatering lead to lush plants which are unsalable. Attention to detail is necessary with Pansies.
- **Pests and diseases:** Aphids become established quickly unless preventative measures are taken. Relatively disease free.
- **Temperature preference:** Pansies like it cool. After establishing seedlings at 45-60° F, drop the temperature to 34-45° F. Light frost at night will not hurt acclimated plants, but growth is slowed considerably. Hard frost is tolerated in garden beds.
- **Light preference:** Full sun. In shadier areas, Pansies may be planted after trees lose their leaves in fall.
- **Special comments:** Many new varieties have recently been developed. This, along with an upsurge in fall gardening interest, is making Pansies a major bedding crop. Well-grown plants are always in demand because Pansies require careful culture and handling to maintain their cheery appearance. This is why chain stores do not sell their fair share.

Peperomia

- **Principal uses:** Indoor foliage plants for medium and high light situations. Mostly smaller plants but very useful in terrariums and combination work. A large number of varieties.
- **Sales potential and season:** Sell reasonably well all year. Main season is November through June as gifts in terrariums or combination planters. Some varieties are suitable for hanging baskets.
- **Propagation methods:** Usually from leaf or stem cuttings. Root quickly at 70-80° F. Do not like high moisture when rooting.

- **Growth in greenhouse or nursery:** Easy to grow and most varieties are reasonably vigorous.
- **Pests and diseases:** No serious pests unless preventive measures are neglected. Stem and leaf rot can be serious if cuttings or plants are overwatered.
- **Temperature preference:** Grow best at 65-70° F, but higher and lower temperatures are tolerated.
- **Light preference:** Strong diffuse light. Will tolerate more and less light but plants are not as attractive.
- **Special comments:** Peperomias are recommended for the year-round operator because they sell reasonably well, have many uses, come in a large variety, and grow quite easily.

Petunia

- **Principal uses:** The premier garden flower for full sun locations. Also extensively used in hanging baskets and patio planters.
- **Sales potential and season:** Extremely popular in sunny climates because it flowers so profusely and a full range of colors is available. New varieties are now available which supposedly will tolerate rather cool winter temperatures in mild climates.
- **Propagation methods:** Almost always from seed which is small but germinates easily and quickly at 65-75° F. Seed must not be allowed to dry out. Some newer varieties are from cuttings.
- **Growth in greenhouse or nursery:** Grows easily and quickly, but tends to become lush and overgrown if too much fertilizer, heat or water is applied. Not an easy crop to grow to perfection.
- **Pests and diseases:** No serious pests if normal precautions are taken. Various stem and leaf rot are serious if damp conditions prevail. Southern growers are particularly plagued by diseases. Botrytis attacks flowers quickly if high humidity prevails.
- **Temperature preference:** Establish seedlings at 55-65° F, then drop the temperature to 45-60° F for finishing. Lower temperatures make it easier to grow compact plants but can lead to disease problems, smaller flowers, and delayed flowering.

- **Light preference:** Full sun. Shade decreases flowering and causes plants to become weak and unacceptably lush.
- **Special comments:** Petunias are perhaps the showiest common garden flower. It is not easy to grow plants to flower in crowded cell pak containers. This is why I prefer to specialize in large hanging baskets and planters where truly spectacular results can be achieved fairly easily. Petunias are good profit makers, but culture and scheduling must be carefully planned.

Poinsettia

- **Principal uses:** The main flower used for decorating during the Christmas season. Mostly in pots but some utilized as cut flowers.
- **Sales potential and season:** Although the sales season is limited to approximately 60 days, many millions of plants are sold nationwide. By offering good plants in a variety of sizes

Poinsettias are in high demand during Christmas.

and colors, there is the potential for an expanded market.
- **Propagation methods:** Commercial production is through cuttings rooted under mist at 70-80° F. Most smaller growers order their rooted cuttings from specialist propagators.
- **Growth in greenhouse or nursery:** Relatively easy and quick if proper environmental conditions are supplied. The large number of new cultivars vary substantially in the exact conditions necessary.
- **Pests and diseases:** White fly is the predominant pest. Clean planting stock and constant preventive measures during growth are absolutely essential. Various stem, root, and flower diseases can also become serious if prevention is neglected.
- **Temperature preference:** Most varieties require 63-68° F for commercial production. Higher and lower temperatures are tolerated, but quality is reduced. Once flowers are mature, the temperature can be dropped to 58-62° F for holding.
- **Light preference:** Full sun in most climates, but extremely sunny conditions may require light shade during establishment of small plants and at flowering. Poinsettias require short days to bloom, and flowering can be delayed or prevented by extraneous sources of light at night.
- **Special comments:** Plenty of lower quality Poinsettias are available for sale at cheap prices. If a good profit is to be made, the smaller grower must concentrate on high quality and a variety of sizes and colors. This crop offers growers the chance for substantial income in midwinter, but it must be managed and priced right to realize a good profit.

Pothos

- **Principal uses:** A semi-vining foliage plant which is utilized extensively for hanging baskets, pots, and combination work.
- **Sales potential and season:** Pothos is perhaps the most widely sold tropical foliage plant. It provides steady sales throughout the year. Often used in large quantities as ground cover for indoor landscaping.
- **Propagation methods:** Cuttings. Root easily at 70-85° F. When large amounts are needed, it is often best to obtain inexpensive starter plants or rooted cuttings from southern growers.

- **Growth in greenhouse or nursery:** An easy grower as long as adequate heat can be maintained. Likes a well-drained soil so roots are not exposed to excess water.
- **Pests and diseases:** Pests are not serious unless preventive measures are ignored. Root rot and various leaf spots can be a problem if there is excess moisture in the soil or around leaf surfaces.
- **Temperature preference:** Pothos will maintain themselves at 60° F but do not make much growth. Good active growth occurs above 70° F. Northern growers have a hard time producing good plants in midwinter unless plenty of heat is available.
- **Light preference:** Lower light can be tolerated, but plants do better when strong diffuse light is available.
- **Special comments:** Although Pothos is difficult to grow profitably in northern greenhouses, it does have a strong and steady demand. Either by producing your plants in summer or purchasing them from southern sources, you can take advantage of this ready market. Southern growers can make steady income by providing high quality products for the northern winter market.

Roses

- **Principal uses:** America's most popular woody garden plant. Used also as patio planters, flowering pot plant, cut flowers.
- **Sales potential and season:** Almost unlimited demand for well-started blooming garden plants in spring and early summer. Plenty of poor quality plants are available, but there is a need for superior quality.
- **Propagation methods:** Usually purchase bare root dormant plants from Rose growing specialists. Suppliers must be chosen carefully to assure that plants are alive and vigorous.
- **Growth in greenhouse or nursery:** Pot and sprout in humid greenhouse or other shelter. Plants grow quickly and easily to the flowering stage if minimum requirements are met.
- **Pests and diseases:** Aphids and spider mites are a problem but can be easily controlled if preventive measures are taken early. Mildew disease is serious if adequate precautions are not taken.

- **Temperature preference:** Grow at 50-60° F. Much lower temperatures can be tolerated once plants are well-established. Significantly higher temperatures promote weak tall growth.
- **Light preference:** Full sun except when dormant plants are being sprouted.
- **Special comments:** Although good dormant plants are expensive and diseases and pests are troublesome, garden Roses can be extremely profitable. The heavy demand means you can price good quality plants at a level considerably above ordinary mass market Roses and still sell a large amount. Cut flowers are a specialty crop for larger growers, overseas imports of cut Roses make this market very competitive.

Shasta Daisy

- **Principal uses:** A popular garden perennial. Can be sold as small starter plants or as large flowering container specimens in early summer.
- **Sales potential and season:** Sells well in spring and summer but somewhat limited in flower color (white). This is the number 1 perennial in some sections of the U.S.
- **Propagation methods:** Usually from seed. Germinates quickly and easily at 55-70° F. Several new varieties have recently been introduced. Choose for flowering date, height, and flower characteristics.
- **Growth in greenhouse or nursery:** One of the easiest perennials to grow, but it is a heavy feeder. Grows so fast it can become overgrown easily so several well-timed crops should be planted.
- **Pests and diseases:** Aphids are a problem if allowed to get started. No serious diseases.
- **Temperature preference:** Will tolerate higher temperatures but prefers 40-50° F for the majority of growing time. If flowering pots are desired, 35-40° F temperatures will enhance bud set.
- **Light preference:** Full sun. Blooming is probably related to day length. Most varieties will not bloom until early summer even if they are old enough. Some new varieties bloom a little earlier.
- **Special comments:** Shasta Daisies perform well for the

consumer. The seasonal display is outstanding, and you can count on good sales when plants are blooming in established landscapes. The ease of culture and relatively brisk demand makes this one of the most profitable perennials. Can be bloomed the first season if started early and grown cool.

Swedish Ivy

- **Principal uses:** An inexpensive indoor foliage plant for high light situations. Sometimes used as a rambling filler in shaded outdoor patio planters and hanging baskets.
- **Sales potential and season:** Swedish Ivy (also known as German Ivy and Creeping Charlie) sells steadily throughout the year because it is one of the best and most vigorous inexpensive foliage plants.
- **Propagation methods:** Cuttings. They root quickly at 55-75° F. This plant is so vigorous that cuttings may be stuck directly to the finishing container without mist or bottom heat.
- **Growth in greenhouse or nursery:** Grows easily and quickly into a dense mound of rambling foliage. Older plants develop long, pendulous branches unless they are pinched back regularly.
- **Pests and diseases:** No serious pests. Stem and leaf rot can be a problem in early growth stages if low temperatures and high humidity prevail.
- **Temperature preference:** Best growth at 60-70° F, but good plants can be produced either side of this range if cultural methods are altered to fit the temperature regime. Several cultivars available. Green is the most popular.
- **Light preference:** High light indoors, shade outdoors. Plants will tolerate some shade indoors but tend to produce longer, less leafy branches.
- **Special comments:** Swedish Ivy has no particular overwhelming advantageous trait, but, when all the factors (reasonable and steady market, insect and disease resistance, rapid easy growth, good appearance, and tolerance of varied conditions) are added together, it becomes an extremely profitable crop for those growers who can sell indoor foliage on year around basis.

Tomatoes, Peppers

- **Principal uses:** Vegetable gardens. Container and raised bed culture. Profitable fruit production indoors is very difficult and is better left to larger, specialized growers.
- **Sales potential and season:** Spring and early summer. Everyone wants to try a Tomato or two each season. Large plants are becoming more popular and can extend the sales season into late summer.
- **Propagation methods:** Seed. Easy to germinate at 70-80° F. Must be removed to cooler temperature and plenty of fresh air as soon as up well or seedlings become elongated. Peppers are susceptible to damping off.
- **Growth in greenhouse or nursery:** Very easy to grow nice crops quickly if a few details are attended to. You must schedule crops carefully to be ready for the relatively short selling season. But they must not be overgrown.
- **Pests and diseases:** Both Tomatoes and Peppers require clean conditions. Although not extremely susceptible to either pests or diseases, a wide range of problems can occur if preventive measures are ignored.
- **Temperature preference:** Grow Tomatoes at 55-65° F after seedlings are established. Peppers like it about 5° F warmer. Higher temperatures will work, but growth is lush. Plants are very susceptible to frost damage.
- **Light preference:** Full sun. Shade will cause unacceptable elongation of stems.
- **Special comments:** You must pay attention to the proper varieties for your climate—repeat business from satisfied customers is important. Choose varieties that are disease resistant. Although diseases may not show up in your greenhouse, they are a major factor in customer disappointment later. An easy crop and big profit maker if you become known for good plants of the proper varieties.

Vinca Vine

- **Principal uses:** As a perennial ground cover vine and as a filler vine in hanging baskets and patio planters. Flowers are blue, but these are seldom the main attraction.

- **Sales potential and season:** Very popular in spring and summer because it is the premier vine used in annual flower combination planters. Can be sold throughout the year as a perennial groundcover in mild climates.
- **Propagation methods:** Cuttings, plant divisions. Tips root quickly if they are not allowed to wilt and are provided with mist.
- **Growth in greenhouse or nursery:** Quick and easy at 45-60° F. Good growth but slower at lower temperatures. Flowers well only if exposed to cool (35-45° F) temperatures in winter.
- **Pests and diseases:** Aphids and spider mites are troublesome unless control measures are practiced. Relatively disease free.
- **Temperature preference:** Very frost tolerant after established. Leaves generally retained through the winter if there is snow protection during the coldest weather.
- **Light preference:** Shade or full sun. Quite tolerant of different light intensities but becomes bunchier in full sun, while shade leads to excessive elongation.
- **Special comments:** Independent garden centers often sell a lot of Vinca Vine simply because the chains do not think to carry it as a separate item. This is one of the garden plants that is not especially showy but almost everyone uses. Sells best if it is sheared back when plants become long and stringy. Several varieties, including common Myrtle which is used as a groundcover.

Viola

- **Principal uses:** Perennial flower beds.
- **Sales potential and season:** A good blooming perennial for early spring and fall. Can be used as a winter annual in milder climates.
- **Propagation methods:** From seed. Germinates easily and quickly at 55-65° F.
- **Growth in greenhouse or nursery:** Grows easily and quickly. Flowers well the first season from seed. Dwarf compact varieties are some of the best blooming early perennials for bedding.

- **Pests and diseases:** Aphids can be a problem if preventive measures are not employed. No serious diseases.
- **Temperature preference:** Grow very cool (33-50° F) after well-established. Will withstand light frost easily or heavy frost after acclimated to the garden.
- **Light preference:** Full sun to very light shade. Shady situations cause elongated, weak growth—too much water, fertilizer, or heat do the same.
- **Special comments:** Violas have the same appeal as Pansies, but flowers are smaller and more numerous. Violas are one of the most suitably hardy perennials for northern areas and can become an important crop if you offer a selection of the best varieties. Seed is generally much cheaper and plants flower earlier than Pansies. A very profitable crop.

Chapter 5

HOW TO MAKE AND SELL PRIVATE LABEL POTTING SOIL WORTH $$THOUSANDS

The title of this chapter may seem somewhat sensationalized. But, I can assure you, my private label potting soil has truly been a gold mine for the past 30 years. And I expect to continue mining this bonanza for many years to come.

My small retail plant store easily sells over $10,000 worth of potting soil every year. Since I manufacture my own brand of soil from very inexpensive ingredients, this means a clear profit of about $7,500.00 each year from selling this product. If this yearly profit is multiplied times the 50 years I expect to be in business, you can see that the resulting lifetime profit is a truly significant sum of $375,000. This is enough money to make a real difference in how enjoyable your life is.

Some of you may wish to point out that similar results could be obtained by selling any brand of potting soil. This is true to some extent, but, as I hope to point out soon, both total sales and the profit percentage with private label potting soils usually far exceed the results of "any old brand."

Private label potting soil represents a small proportion of total merchandise sales for my business, but the profits it generates are 2-3 times what can be reasonably expected from other product lines of similar sales volume.

This chapter will be somewhat more detailed than previous ones because the specialized information is not (to my knowledge) available from any other source, and there is a good amount of specific data you need in order to assure that your private label potting soil becomes a true goldmine. All the details are included because I consider them an integral part of the whole concept; please carefully consider any changes you make, and try to estimate how they may affect the total program. A wise person always evaluates whether or not some changes are appropriate under their unique business and production conditions, but only a fool pays for information and then fails to utilize it to the fullest extent possible.

The information in this chapter will generate exceptional profits over the years, and it will allow you to realize these profits quickly, easily, and surely—but you must study the details carefully, and make sure each step is implemented in a responsible manner. I have spent the better part of my adult life learning how to make money from all types of activity involving ornamental plants, and some of the lessons I learned by trial and error were extremely expensive. In this chapter, I am offering you one of my very best money making programs—but only you can carry it to completion.

A bit of explanation concerning the word "soil" is in order before we proceed further. Natural garden

Private label potting soil is an excellent supplemental source of income.

or field soil is seldom used nowadays as the major ingredient for growing ornamental container plants. The potting medias generally in use at present are made from a combination of ingredients (natural soil may be one of those chosen), which, when blended together, provide better plant growing conditions than could be obtained with most natural soils. The reasons for this switch to "modified" soils are rather involved—but most importantly they allow plants to grow more uniformly and vigorously in containers and restricted garden areas. The potting soils mentioned later are representative of the blended "modified" type.

WHY IS PRIVATE LABEL POTTING SOIL BETTER?

Selling potting soil in your plant related business can be very profitable. But it is important for you to understand why personally manufactured potting soils can be much more profitable than selling ordinary brands available from commercial producers.

First and foremost among the reasons is that you can generally make a much better product for customers at less than 1/2 the cost of commercial brands. This is the main reason I began manufacturing my own potting soil over 30 years ago. My customers are happier because their plants grow better, and I am pleased because I pocket all the savings realized in manufacturing and shipping. Transportation to your store from distant sources can often add 40% to the cost of bulky and heavy potting soils. If you use locally available ingredients, this shipping cost can be trimmed to the point of being negligible.

Incidentally, after my customers became convinced that our private label soil was much better, I raised the price considerably over that of common commercial brands—thereby increasing my profit margin to the point where it is almost ridiculous. And customers still happily purchase tons of it because it really is superior. This soil is such a good deal for me that, given a choice, I would rather make it than grow plants.

In addition, manufacturing potting soil on-site gives you complete control over a product line which is important to your overall business success. When purchasing commercial brands, you will often find that certain ones are out of stock at times when you could be selling a lot— or they may be short of sizes needed—thereby reducing your sales volume. And worse yet, after convincing customers that a certain brand is good—it may become unavailable. When it comes to potting soil, it makes good business sense to assure yourself of a convenient and steady supply of high quality products. You can accomplish this goal with a minimum of expense and work.

Over and above the goodwill private label potting soil can generate because it is a superior plant growing medium, it will also enhance your professional image among customers. They naturally assume that all your plants and products are of equal caliber. This customer loyalty quickly translates into bigger profits for your entire business. And, if you prominently label all bags as being a product of your home county or town, many people will purchase simply because they prefer to support local industry.

Finally, you can use potting soil containers to advertise your plant business. This is done directly by making sure the main drawing points of your business are prominently mentioned on the bags. A good product label with detailed and accurate directions about how to use the soil and how to grow good plants is an indirect advertising avenue; customers will appreciate the extra care which you have given towards solving their problems.

Eventually, you may be so successful with potting soil that you start thinking about selling it to other plant stores and mass merchandisers. While this may or may not be an appropriate action in your particular circumstances, I caution you to think it over carefully before going this route. Most of the advantages listed here for private label potting soils are valid as they relate to individual plant businesses or small chains of stores which specialize in plant products. The large chain stores are primarily interested in a cheap product which can be shipped to all their stores. Even if the chain buyers knew what good potting soil was, they would probably worry more about price than quality.

Long ago I experimented with selling my potting soil to large stores in a number of states. Without going into details, this project was not worth the headaches it created. I have since been content with reaping the good profits potting soil generates at my own retail business. Sometimes I take on additional wholesale business from florists and garden stores that come to purchase plants from my greenhouse, but only if they are interested in purchasing good soil at a price which is profitable to me.

POSSIBLE POTTING SOIL HEADACHES

Although private label potting soil is a good business project for almost anyone who already owns or who will be starting a plant related business, there are a few potential problems which should be brought to your attention. Most of the difficulties mentioned are quite minor and can be solved simply by being aware of them as you make plans; a few problems are more serious but still rather easily solved by several hours work and a small monetary outlay.

Please carefully address each of the points mentioned below since even minor difficulties can eventually become major problems if they are not attended to properly. Some may even cause the failure of an otherwise sound program. Also understand that there may be potential problems or regulations which I have never encountered; you must be aware that unanticipated situations and circumstances arise from time to time.

Developing a private label potting soil program should be thought of as a long term project. It will probably become a good profit center for many years to come; therefore, you should be very conscientious with each detail of manufacturing and marketing, and you should devote

Front Design Sample
The actual bag is in four-color print.
This is the smallest weight bag I make.

JOHNNY APPLESEED GREENHOUSES

ALL-PURPOSE

POTTING SOIL

Garden soil should not be added to Johnny Appleseed Potting Soil when potting indoor plants. Seeds and cuttings may be started in potting soil but superior results are obtained with our especially formulated JOHNNY APPLESEED SEED GERMINATION AND CUTTING STARTER MIX.

PLANTING INSTRUCTIONS

1. MOISTEN LIGHTLY and mix potting soil thoroughly prior to use.
2. WASH POTS to be used with soap and hot water then rinse thoroughly.
3. ADEQUATE DRAINAGE is important to plant growth. Cover drainage hole of pot with large clean pebbles. Only plants requiring little water such as cacti will grow for long periods in containers with no drain holes. If no drainage is available, water must never be applied heavily enough to collect in the bottom of pots.
4. DECORATIVE POTTERY with no drainage may be used by putting plants in growing pots with drainage and slipping it into the decorative piece. Place a 1-2 inch layer of coarse gravel on the bottom of the decorative pot for the growing pot to rest on. If water accumulates in the bottom of your decorative pot, then slip out growing pot immediately and empty excess water.
5. ADD SOME POTTING SOIL to the bottom of the new pot and push root ball firmly into it, making sure that previous soil level is at least ½ inch below the top of the pot.
6. FILL AROUND EDGES of root ball pressing new soil firmly into place with fingertips. Generally, plants should not be planted deeper than the old soil level.
7. WATER LIGHTLY after potting and do not water again until soil surface becomes slightly dry. Avoid direct sunlight for a few days after repotting.

JOHNNY APPLESEED TIPS FOR HEALTHY PLANTS

1. CONSULT A PLANT BOOK for specific cultural practices for each variety.
2. SMALL AMOUNTS OF FERTILIZERS are needed by all plants. When plants begin to show new leaves and sprouts, begin a regular feeding program according to directions on the label. Never add more than recommended.
3. OVERWATERING KILLS PLANTS. Most plants prefer to be watered well and not watered again until the soil surface becomes slightly dry to the touch. Never allow plants to stand in water.
4. EVERY 3-6 MONTHS your plant should be watered heavily from the top of the pot until water drips freely from the drain hole. This water carries out excess salts accumulated from city water and unused fertilizer.
5. SUDDEN TEMPERATURE CHANGES damage plants. Position plants away from door areas, heat and air conditioning ducts.

Label Sample

Use this as a guide if you wish.

Note: I make no mention of food or plant fertilizer.

adequate research to assure success. In many cases, the information you need may be presented here, but some of you will undoubtedly need to implement additional or alternative methods in order to develop the most successful program possible for specific circumstances.

Develop strategy

The first thing you should do when developing a private label potting soil program is to think out a coherent and sensible strategy of operation. Basically, this means you must be sure of what you want to do and how you plan to accomplish it. Every operation is unique to some degree simply because circumstances vary slightly at different times and places. Use the information given here as a guide for developing your strategy, but always remember that you must fine tune each aspect of your personal circumstances. A poorly conceived basic strategy can nullify every future action.

The customer is king

Although there are many reasons why you should consider implementing a private label potting soil program, no aspect is more important than making sure the product pleases your customers. You can never make a long term profit (much less big profits) unless the ultimate user is happy.

Basically, this means your potting soil must grow better plants than any other product they have used. It must also look and feel good, and it must be available in sizes and formulations which meet their needs. You must provide adequate information which allows your customers to conveniently use the product in a proper manner.

Government regulations

Everyone is aware that governmental regulations affect all aspects of our lives—even down to the level of plain old "dirt." Yes, you must comply with various laws and rules when you manufacture and sell potting soil. Most of these regulations are promulgated by your own state government, but there may be occasions when federal laws are involved (the latter case is true generally only if your soil contains a federally regulated substance such as soil pesticides).

I will point out the most likely regulatory areas which you should investigate but you must understand I am not a qualified expert in all 50 states. It is ultimately your responsibility to make sure you are completely meeting all regulatory obligations.

Generally, the state department of agriculture is responsible for administrating the laws governing potting soil and fertilizers. But, to be safe, you should be sure to ask that agency if there may be other departments to contact. Some states have separate departments of weights and measures which are responsible for assuring that all products are accurately represented in that respect.

Be thorough in checking out possible regulations which may apply—the ones you know about ahead of time are generally easy to comply with or to avoid altogether by using alternate methods of manufacture or packaging. But the ones which surprise you could prove extremely troublesome once you have already begun a particular method of production.

The state of Georgia is the only one I know of which has enacted a set of comprehensive laws governing potting soils and related products. Other states may soon follow.

Most states have only a few basic rules which are sometimes haphazardly enforced—but don't take a chance: learn the requirements and comply with them. In most cases it is relatively easy and inexpensive to do so, and the laboratory information you must provide for documentation is often very helpful for your own information. The question of laboratory tests will be discussed in more detail later.

One aspect of potting soils which is sometimes troublesome from a regulatory standpoint is that of the nutrient (fertilizer) content. Most states are very careful to regulate what they consider to be plant foods or fertilizers, and most also require that you have a license to legally transact business in these products. But the several states in which I have done business have only minimal laws concerning potting soil (mostly concerned with accurate measurement). Therefore, it makes sense to avoid any reference to fertilizer or plant food in your advertising or upon labels. By using slightly different wording, you may be able to avoid significant regulations and the expense of purchasing a license. The only way you can positively be certain in this respect is to obtain a copy of the pertinent regulations and read them carefully—this is simply a word game, but you must take it seriously to avoid trouble in the future.

As regards weights and measures, I always weigh every bag of potting soil we produce—but in order to avoid purchasing an expensive state approved scale, workers are instructed to add 10% extra product over what the bag states. This assures that the customer gets more than bargained for and allows production employees to weigh more quickly. This strategy saves time, gives the customer extra soil, and satisfies the regulators. Everyone is happy.

The ingredients are so inexpensive that I save money because it takes less time to weigh the sacks.

If you wish to measure and represent your soil by volume, please be aware that potting soil can expand or contract significantly in shipment, storage, and display. Therefore, you may measure it carefully by volume but still be in violation of the laws when state personnel perform their measurement. I prefer to weigh because there is little chance of weight deviation once the soil is inside a plastic bag which prevents moisture loss.

You should avoid the use of soil pesticides or fungicides in any potting soils. This is the "kiss of death" because you immediately become subject to regulation by the federal EPA (Environmental Protection Agency). Complying with their rules is generally very expensive so that only larger companies which specialize in pesticide production can afford the cost.

There are valid reasons for incorporating pesticides and fungicides into soil under certain situations, but none of them make practical or economic sense as regards private label potting soils intended for general public use.

One other subject which you should be aware of is that of trademark infringement. Don't deliberately copy some other product's name, especially if it relates in some way to plants or soil. If you simply must use a name you know has been used previously, check carefully to be sure it has not been trademarked or copyrighted. This is an involved process and can often be expensive.

Unknowingly choosing a trademarked name is unlikely unless you consciously try to do so. If this happens by chance, it is even more unlikely that it will be noticed if your soil is used only locally. In the extremely improbable event that someone objects to your accidental trademark infringement, you will have to agree to change the name on your labels.

Making potting soil can be dusty and dirty work. Be sure to take at least rudimentary precautions for your own and your workers' health. Don't mix powder dry soil so that the dust becomes dangerous. And make sure that everyone wears safety glasses if there is any chance that dirt may enter the eye. Some ingredients like perlite must be handled more carefully to avoid the entry of airborne particles into the lungs. Use your common sense! If you mix soil in large amounts on a more or less daily basis, you should develop a detailed safety plan for all workers who are directly involved in the process.

The problem of profit

Even if your potting soil is the best there is, it will not be a success unless it is manufactured, priced, and marketed in a manner which yields a good profit. I will touch upon some manufacturing costs and pricing details here, and then finish up the subject when marketing aspects are discussed at the end of the chapter.

Totaling up the manufacturing costs is relatively straight forward. Simply get together all the costs for materials, bags, labor, facilities, and machines you use, and then determine how much these items cost per bag of soil produced. I find the easiest way to do this is to make up a reasonable size batch of about 100 bags of soil, then add up the total cost of producing that batch. This cost divided by the exact number of bags produced will equal your production cost per bag.

Don't forget to add a development cost into your totals. The price of this book, your time spent studying it, and any other preliminary expenses such as laboratory testing, licenses, and time spent complying with regulations should all be charged off as a development cost. Some guess work is involved in this process because, although you may be able to determine total development costs rather accurately, it is difficult to say how much of this cost should be attributed to each batch or each bag. Usually, I just take the total development cost and divide it by a rough guess of how many bags will be produced in the first 2 years. This gives development cost per bag for the first 2 years of production, after which you may want to eliminate this category from your cost estimates, or just leave it in and pocket the extra money as one of the many benefits of your labors.

It may also be a little difficult to arrive at accurate figures for the cost of facilities since you will probably use some existing building which you own or rent. After all, it only takes a few hours to make several hundred bags of soil—there is no need to have a special building for this job. In this case, just charge a daily or hourly facilities fee against each batch of soil you make.

Labor will most likely be the largest cost so be sure you spend adequate time in finding out exactly how much per hour to charge for it. And always be sure you charge a fair hourly wage for any work you or your family contributes towards making soil.

All through this chapter I have been assuming that readers either operate or will operate a plant or garden related business—in other words, I assume you have a means of selling the potting soil you produce. It doesn't make much sense (on the retail level particularly) to set up an entire business specifically to sell potting soil. This activity is meant simply as a profitable addition to your main business of selling plants or plant related material.

I mention this mainly in order to be certain every reader knows how this information should be interpreted (as a means of adding a profitable product line, not as a stand alone business) but also so that you become aware that normal marketing costs are associated with your potting soil program. If you are to realize a profit, you must "mark up" your soil at the wholesale level (production) and again at the retail level.

If the cost of production is $1.00 per bag, then I charge $2.00 when selling wholesale and $4.00 when selling retail. In other words, I want to double my cost of production and double my cost of purchasing soil from myself. This "mark up" structure has proven profitable to me over the years, but you may want to use a different "mark up." Your "mark ups" should provide adequate room for marketing costs plus a healthy profit.

When you both produce and then sell the soil at retail, you are entitled to a profit at *both* the wholesale and retail levels. Only you can determine what "mark up" is sufficient for your particular operation, but, personally, I don't like to work for peanuts, and I refuse to accept less "mark up" than was mentioned above.

Realizing a decent profit on your potting soil should not be a problem if you diligently study the costs involved, apply the proper "mark ups," and restrict your marketing to the retail situations I have mentioned. If you want to sell large volumes to other dealers at wholesale, then you may encounter difficulties obtaining a high enough price to make the project a money maker. Many wholesale buyers will not pay the price you need. As mentioned previously, my advice is to restrict your wholesale activity to smaller stores that recognize the quality of your product and are willing to pay the price you ask.

Miscellaneous considerations

Let's quickly summarize some final points which should help your potting soil operation run more smoothly and profitably.

When deciding which ingredients to use in soil, try to choose materials which are in your normal business inventory. For example, if you own a greenhouse and use peat moss regularly, then utilize it for potting soil in preference to some other organic matter source which is not readily available on a daily basis.

Set up your soil operation to be as flexible as possible. In other words, don't purchase expensive machines, millions of bags, or hire a full time crew of workers. These actions lock you into rigid operational methods and big overhead costs which reduce the ability to change things later as you learn more about the business.

Your soil making process should be designed so that ordinary workers can easily step in and begin production. Eliminate complicated procedures which require specialized knowledge. You want the whole process to be as automatic as possible in the future so you don't have to be around to supervise the making of every bag.

Finally, pay attention to quality control aspects such as weeds, diseases, and moisture content. If you aren't careful, weed seed and various diseases can easily be introduced via the ingredients or sloppy manufacturing methods. And the moisture content of soil can fluctuate wildly unless steps are taken to control it. This is important because moisture content affects the storage qualities and appearance of the product. It will also affect the weight of bags considerably.

THE FIRST STEPS

Before you begin making potting soil, there are several decisions and preliminary steps which should be carefully considered. Some of these have been mentioned previously, but it will be helpful to summarize them now.

- Make sure you have a detailed marketing plan. Project how, when, where, and how much soil you will be selling. Some of this information will be reasonably well known, but some of it will be only an educated guess. However, a thoughtful estimate is better than no thought at all.
- Decide all of the major functions which your potting soils and related products must perform for customers. In other words what will customers be using them for? Growing house plants? Growing garden plants? Seed germination? Cutting production? etc.
- Based upon these major functions, what different types of soil and related products do you need to offer? And in what size packages do you need to offer them? What will be the price of each type and size?
- Locate sources for and choose the sizes and types of soil bags you will need. Get them locally if possible. The better quality zip-lock bags and compactor bags may be suitable if you don't plan large production runs. Most towns will have a distributor who can supply you with all sizes and strengths of plastic bags, and you will want to use these more specialized bags if you plan to sell a considerable amount of soil. Every large city has manufacturers and major wholesalers of every type bag you might need; look in the Yellow Pages.

   Generally, you will want to use standard bags unless you plan extremely large production runs of soil. I have contracted bag manufacturers to design and produce special bags for my

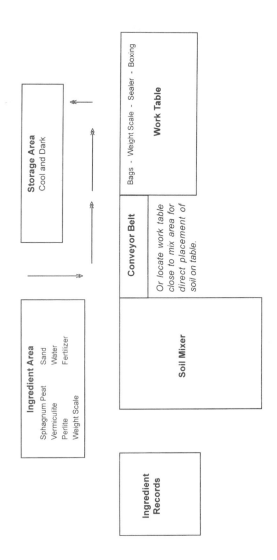

Sample diagram of soil manufacturing layout.

Entire area should be cleared to avoid contact with weed seeds, plant debris and other contamination. Examine mixers, conveyors, heat sealers, and all other equipment for safety hazards.

Peat moss supply stack.

line of soil—these bags make the product look much nicer. But this is an expensive process initially, and you won't want to consider it until you know exactly what your needs will be. In order to get these special bags at a good price, I must often order a production run that may last for 5 years. This means I can't change sizes or design for that period of time without discarding my previous bag inventory.

The company listed below can supply you with various types of soil bags at reasonable prices—they aren't the cheapest, but they do not require large production runs either. I use them for special sizes for which I will not need large numbers.

Mansfield Bag and Paper Company
P.O. Box 1414
Mansfield, OH 44901
Tel: 1-800-654-8654 or (419)525-2814
Fax: (419)522-6942

There are several technical considerations about bags of which you should be aware. Of course you want the cheapest bag possible, but it must fulfill certain requirements. Is it strong enough? Will you be able to seal it easily and quickly? Does it resist degradation from sunlight (this is important if soil will be displayed outdoors for long periods)? Is it always available? Is it suitable for the labels you plan to use?

- Developing a good label for your soil is an important long term consideration. Your label not only provides the initial impulse for consumers to notice the soil, it is the means by which you convey all the necessary information about how to use the product properly. This information will, in large part, determine how successful customers are in growing their plants—and how happy they are with your soil.

A reduced size black and white representation of the label I use on one of my soil products was previously shown. This label is printed right on the bag, but, initially, you will probably want to order gummed labels which you can stick to the bag. This is a cheaper and more flexible way of getting started. Your instructions can be enclosed in a small plastic envelope which is tied to the bag or which is stuck to the bag. All these items are readily available locally from print shops and stationary stores.

MAKING POTTING SOIL SUCCESSFULLY

The information given below provides the basic criteria to use when choosing potting soil ingredients, and it gives actual step-by-step instructions for manufacturing specific soils which might be utilized in your program. Some of this information is based upon common sense and can be modified to suit individual circumstances. Other aspects of the information, particularly as it relates to soil formulas, is based upon physical and chemical properties of soil ingredients and should not be modified without reference to the underlying technical principles. An easily understood summary of these technical principles is contained in *The Greenhouse And Nursery Handbook* in chapters dealing with soil, fertilizers, and water. I urge you to study this book before initiating any potting soil project because it will give you a good general background to interpret how your soil can affect plant growth. If you plan to modify any of the following formulas, *The Greenhouse And Nursery Handbook* should definitely be consulted for proper guidelines.

Choosing ingredients

Many of the criteria which should be used to choose ingredients for your potting soil are sprinkled throughout this chapter. A brief summary here, however, will get them fixed firmly in mind before we consider actual ingredients and manufacturing.

- Ingredients must have properties which lead to superior plant growth when used under the intended circumstances.
- Must be safe to use individually or in combination with other ingredients and fulfill all laws, rules, and regulations.
- Should be economical to purchase.
- Constant availability of ingredients in uniform quality grades is an important consideration.
- How the soil looks and feels to customers is important. Ingredients should be chosen to enhance the visual and tactile properties of the finished product.
- Both the individual ingredients and the resulting soil must be physically and chemically stable (will not change or degrade appreciably) under prolonged storage (at least 6 months).
- Should have properties which do not impede or complicate the manufacturing process.

Locating ingredients

All the necessary ingredients can be easily purchased from wholesale distributors of greenhouse and nursery supplies. If you cannot locate one of these firms in or near your town by using the Yellow Pages, then I would suggest that you purchase a copy of the Andmar Press *Guidebook to Wholesale Sources.*

If you already operate a greenhouse or nursery, it is likely you have most of the suggested ingredients (or a suitable substitute) in your inventory. This is one reason making potting soil to sell is so profitable for most people who grow plants commercially.

Since prices can vary widely, always check out 2 or 3 sources of supply for ingredients. And don't forget to find out how much freight costs will be—this can be very important in total manufacturing costs. Most potting soil formulas are based upon the major ingredient being sphagnum peat or composted bark. One or the other of these is almost always available in a suitable quality from local discount stores (especially when on sale). Unless you purchase peat or bark in truckload quantities for your basic greenhouse or nursery business, these local discount store sources may be the most economical place to purchase these particular supplies.

Alternative ingredients

I have already made reference to the fact that modification and substitution of soil ingredients should be carefully planned. You must have adequate information in order to modify or substitute properly.

One alternative to mixing your own soil formula is to purchase large quantities of pre-mixed commercial growing media. These mixes are supplied by numerous manufacturers. Sources can be found in *The Guidebook to Wholesale Sources.* These commercial growing mixes range from occasionally poor, to mostly adequate, up to occasionally excellent. Just because you purchase them from *supposed* experts does not mean you are relieved of all responsibility for determining if they are what your customers need and want.

Commercial mixes are not cheap (usually at least double the cost of mixing your own soil), but they may be advantageous in certain circumstances. If your state requires extensive and continued testing of soil properties and an expensive annual license, it may be possible to simply purchase large quantities of soil from a licensed manufacturer and repackage it in smaller bags with your brand name or retail store name. The manufacturer may even allow you to continue using their brand name and ingredient list while simply affixing your store name to the bags with a label. In this case, you would almost certainly not have to separately meet state regulations.

I'm sure you can easily see the downside of using commercial bulk soil for making your product. It costs a lot more and it is not blended to meet your special needs. Also, you are relying for supply upon a manufacturer who may or may not be in business next year or who may change the formula at any time.

BASIC SOIL FORMULAS

Recipes for potting soils and other basic plant or seed mixes are given below. These have worked well for me over many years and have provided excellent results under most circumstances. But just because they work for me doesn't mean they are perfect for you. Evaluate and test them much like you would any commercially available mix. You have the final responsibility for determining if these recipes meet all the criteria for plant growth, safety, and compliance with regulators.

Here are a few important comments about these recipes which you should digest carefully.

- They contain only a minimal amount of fertilizers (just enough to get plants off to a healthy start—then the grower must supply adequate mineral or organic fertilizers for continued growth).
- They are on the lower end (somewhat acid) of the recommended pH scale; this is because the ongoing fertilizers which I generally recommend are often at the high end of the pH scale and most water sources are at the high end also (thus the low original soil pH tends to be balanced eventually by additions of fertilizer and water which are higher in pH).
- No micronutrients (chemical elements needed in very small quantities for plant growth) are added to these mixes because natural impurities present in the ingredients and in irrigation water generally provide enough for initial growth. Be sure the ongoing fertilizers you recommend to customers contain micronutrients (they will be listed on the label).
- I have occasionally experimented with composted bark as a substitute for the peat moss in these formulas and found no harmful effect. But composted bark quality is notoriously variable from source to source, and I do not recommend substitution of it in place of sphagnum peat moss unless there is a compelling reason—even then, the effects of the substitution upon plant growth and development should be carefully tested and analyzed.
- No soil sterilizing chemicals or techniques are employed because if high grade and clean ingredients are used the resulting soil (although not truly sterile) is clean enough from weeds and diseases for all practical purposes. You must inspect ingredients carefully in this regard.

Suggested mix for outdoor garden use

This soil mix is recommended as one which can be used in the pure form for growing plants in containers outdoors or as a mixture with natural garden soil for outdoor containers and restricted garden areas. This mix is the least expensive of those which will be listed and thus is often more appropriate when larger quantities of soil are used for outdoor purposes. It has also proven to be a good general purpose soil for commercial greenhouses and nurseries. This dual purpose capability is very useful in that retail potting soil can be produced almost daily as needed from the greenhouse or nursery stockpile. The pH of this formula is decidedly acid (low)—it is best if fertilizers used after potting with the pure mix are of a basic or alkaline nature (high pH). Limestone can be incorporated at mixing time to raise the pH.

2 compressed bales sphagnum peat (3.8 cubic feet each)
11 cubic feet washed sand (mortar sand)
18 ounces triple superphosphate
5 ounces potassium nitrate (dissolve in 5 gallons of water and distribute evenly)

Suggested mix for general purpose indoor plant use

This mix is good for almost every type of indoor foliage plant, as it is the one which relates to the sample directions shown earlier. It can also be used as a good greenhouse, nursery, or outdoor potting soil, but it is more expensive due to the perlite added. The perlite lets water drain through more readily and also cuts down on the soil weight. The lime is added in order to adjust the pH upward so that customers need not worry greatly if they use an acid reaction fertilizer after potting. Most types of seed that consumers generally handle can be germinated in it easily, but I will also give you a formula which is meant specifically for seed germination.

2 compressed bales sphagnum peat (3.8 cubic feet each)
5 cubic feet washed sand (mortar sand)

4 cubic feet perlite coarse grind (coarser than 6 mesh)
5 pounds calcium carbonate lime
15 ounces triple superphosphate
5 ounces potassium nitrate (dissolve in 5 gallons of water and
    distribute evenly)

Suggested seed germination and cutting mix

These formulas are special purpose ones which you likely will not need to offer on a retail basis unless a real demand is perceived. I do not sell a large enough retail volume of them to justify making special labels. But I will list the ingredients just in case you have a need. The first formula is for vegetative cuttings and coarser seed, while the second is for fine seed such as raw Petunia, Begonia, and Portulaca seed.

2 compressed bales sphagnum peat (3.8 cubic feet each)
8 cubic feet coarse grind perlite (coarser than 6 mesh)
4 pounds ground limestone (calcium carbonate)
5 ounces potassium nitrate
15 ounces triple superphosphate

The second formula is the same except 6 cubic feet of fine mesh vermiculite is substituted for the perlite. Peat should be finely ground.

Pure form ingredients sometimes requested by customers

Each of the following pure ingredients can sometimes be sold in reasonable volume during the season when people are starting their own garden seeds. There is usually no need to label the bags because demand lasts for only a short while and because the customer generally knows what to look for or they ask for it specifically by name.

- Perlite—Coarse grade

- Vermiculite—Be sure it is horticultural grade rather than construction grade.
- Washed sand—This is ordinary mortar sand available at local sand and gravel companies. Be sure to use a strong bag if you offer sand for sale.
- Sphagnum peat—You will likely offer big bales of this already, but some people want small packages, even if the price is high for the volume.

Cautions about ingredients

In order to produce excellent potting soil which does the proper job for your customers, you must select high quality ingredients and utilize them properly. Listed below are some of the more important points concerning this step.

- Be sure the peat moss you purchase is labeled as *sphagnum* moss. To be certain the brand you utilize is essentially free of weed seed, moisten a large sample well and let it sit in an open cakepan (approximately 12 inches by 12 inches square and 2 inches deep) for 3 weeks at approximately 70° F. If you get more than 1 or 2 weeds germinating in this square foot of surface area, try another brand.
- The washed sand (mortar sand) you use should also be free of weeds—perform the same test as above. Sand should not contain appreciable quantities of silt, clay, or gravel. Make sure the sand company does not add any chemicals to the sand you purchase—there are some cases where special additives are used to make concrete and mortar cure better. Ask questions!
- Perlite and vermiculite should be purchased from a reliable horticultural dealer who can assure you that it is of a quality which can safely be used with plants. The same sources and assurances should be required for all fertilizers and amendments introduced into your soil.
- Triple superphosphate is supplied to the suggested mixes in luxury amounts. The dosage could be cut in half if the soils were not to be grown in for long periods of time or if a fertilizer containing phosphorous was used after plants began good growth. Extra phosphorous is not harmful to plants unless

especially large overdoses are supplied. If you cannot obtain triple superphosphate, single superphosphate will suffice but it must be added in **double** the amount required for triple superphosphate.

- The fertilizers and soil amendments suggested remain chemically stable for reasonably long periods in the mixes. **Do not substitute** other ingredients unless you **know** they also will remain stable. Of course, they must also be appropriate in regard to other essential properties. If you are an ecology buff and wish to use organic fertilizer sources, be warned that organic fertilizers generally are extremely unstable chemically when mixed into moist soil and stored. Some of the possible chemical changes occurring can be harmful to plant growth.

- Be careful when measuring fertilizers—do not guess. Potassium nitrate is an especially concentrated fertilizer— strong overdoses can be extremely harmful to plants. In addition, it is an oxidizer—this means it can help combustibles burn more violently, and, under certain rare circumstances, it can cause explosions. Read the cautions on the label carefully and provide proper storage. I have handled this fertilizer daily in large quantities for over 25 years and never had even a slight problem, so it isn't anything like dealing with high explosives: you should simply handle it according to directions.

- If your state has regulations against the addition of **any** amount of fertilizer or plant food to potting soils (whether or not the addition is noted on the label), you might consider leaving all these types of ingredients out of your soil and recommend that customers use the proper amount of a readily available commercial fertilizer to feed their plants (they can either blend it in the soil immediately before use or water with it right after planting). Liquid formulations are generally best. Needless to say, you should carry a good stock of the particular brand you recommend, and it should be one which you know works well. This route is also a good method to employ if you strongly prefer to use only organic fertilizer formulations.

The manufacturing process

Now we are ready to discuss the actual soil mixing and bagging process. Most of the steps here are common sense suggestions, but I will list them in the order which they most likely should be performed so that you have a handy checklist to work from.

- Before starting, design a simple work process or flow chart for the area in which you will be working. Be sure to include any safety precautions you feel necessary.
- Set up in a handy area where you can work quickly. It must be clean so that weeds, trash, and other contamination have no chance of getting in your soil.
- It is best to mix soil in a machine designed to blend soil, but old cement mixers are fine if you take precautions to assure mixing is done properly. Mixing by hand or shovel is okay too, although it is lots of work. Mix all ingredients thoroughly but not to the point where the structure of certain ingredients is destroyed. Perlite and vermiculite are prone to break up into overly fine particles if mixed too long.
- Blend in fertilizers as the mixing occurs, but do it with common sense: don't dump everything in one spot. Spread it evenly—this is important. Check the fertilizer bags twice to make sure you have the right formulation.
- List all ingredients and quantities for each batch of soil as you mix it up, then double check the list before you finish to make sure everything is included in the proper amounts.
- Add water to the mix until it feels slightly moist to the touch. It is best for it to seem just a little drier at this point than you might like because as the soil sits for a few hours, it tends to feel slightly more moist. When you pick up a handful and squeeze it tightly in your fist, no water should drip out—that would be too wet.

    Moist soil is easier to use for planting, and customers like the feel of it better than totally dry soil. However, excessive moisture will make the bags sweat a great deal and can promote the growth of algae and fungi. Retail potting soil is best left as dry as possible, as long as it is wet enough to appeal to customers and plants can be potted easily. When soil is selling quickly and will be in the bags no more than a week or two, it can be moistened more heavily.

- Moist soil is heavy and bulky. If you are going to process larger amounts, a conveyor system is often a good investment.

- When the soil is on your processing table, don't let it lie there loose for more than a few hours. Long delays in bagging can cause inconsistencies in moisture content and, consequently, in the weight of bags.

- As the bags are filled, each one is weighed quickly. My employees are instructed to overfill bags by approximately 10% to avoid the possibility that some bags may turn out slightly under the weight stated on bags.

- Seal bags securely. Whether you use heat seals, zip-locks, or tie them in some manner, the sealing job should withstand all normal handling without allowing soil to leak out. Leaky bags can become a real nuisance when placed in your store. A few bags in every batch should be checked for proper sealing.

- Once the bags are sealed, punch a couple of holes in the plastic bag with small diameter stiff wire, then squeeze the bag firmly to remove excess air. Too much air in the bags makes them hard to stack in displays.

- As the bagging process is finished, take care to keep the outside of bags reasonably clean. Although people are buying "dirt," they don't like to start getting dirty until the proper time—when they begin gardening.

- Store your soil in a cool, dark place until it is time for display. All the formulas listed in this book can be stored for up to 6 months without appreciable chemical change.

Testing soil for quality

Your soil can be tested for quality by two means: 1) Biologically, and 2) In the laboratory. Each method has particular strengths, weaknesses, and applications.

Biological testing means that you actually grow plants in the soil, observe the results, and make conclusions about how the soil affected growth and development. You can easily perform valid biological tests without specialized equipment. The most important things you must do are to carefully plan the experiments ahead of time, control the experimental conditions so that the information you desire is produced, and interpret the results only from the experimental data—not from what you would like to happen. These plant growth tests show exactly how well your soils perform.

Laboratory soil tests are performed to determine the exact ingredient contents and physical and chemical properties. These tests are essential, at least in the beginning, so that you can use the results to fine tune or adjust soil properties to the approximate ranges you desire. They are also essential if your state requires an independent analysis of soil ingredients and properties.

Laboratory tests do not tell you how well plants will actually grow in the soil, but they do allow you to predict how well plants *should* grow in it. A biological growth test is necessary to confirm the expectations predicted from lab tests. Both biological and laboratory tests should be repeated at least once a year to make sure no significant changes have occurred in the soils you produce.

The formulas which I have suggested in this chapter are tested biologically on a constant basis in our greenhouses and nursery, but the final responsibility for testing rests with you. I can only say that, under our conditions, they perform superbly.

Selling potting soil successfully

The potting soil you produce will be worthless unless you can sell it profitably. We have already covered topics dealing with how you might sell soil and how to price it, but we need to further examine some merchandising methods in your own store.

- Keep your soil displays neat and adequately stocked at all times.
- Display a reasonable amount of soil even in the slow times of year—this will remind customers that you have what they want when they do need it.
- Use the best high traffic display areas for your private label soil—remember, it is a high profit item. You want to sell as much as possible!
- The high profit nature of your soil justifies setting up multiple display areas in different parts of the store. Be sure there is one at the check out counter!
- Don't run out of soil during the busy gardening season. After all, this is one of the main reasons you are making private label soil—to assure a constant supply. You can lose 50% of yearly sales volume by being out of stock during the peak gardening months.
- Keep your soil out of the direct sun as much as possible. Heat and light tends to degrade the bags and can cause algae and fungal growth in the soil. Chemical changes in the soil are also accelerated.
- Bring attention to your soil. Use signs to communicate the benefits it supplies to customers. And instruct all employees to actively sell your soil whenever they make a related sale. You will be surprised at the increased volume if you have a definite program of tie-in selling.
- Offer soil in appropriate sizes. People using soil outside for potting or gardening will want larger bags. They generally want less for indoor plants. The smallest size I offer is approximately equal to 1/2 gallon in volume, while the largest size is 5 gallons. Bags larger than this are too heavy for most people to handle easily, so I just offer 2 bags at a slight discount.

PART II

HOW TO FIND A GOOD JOB WORKING WITH PLANTS, TREES, AND FLOWERS

Chapter 1

INTRODUCTION TO EMPLOYMENT IN HORTICULTURE

As a commercial grower of ornamental plants, I have hired hundreds of people. And I have interviewed a much larger number for prospective employment. In some cases the unpleasant task of "firing" certain individuals has also been my responsibility.

Since my continued success in commercial horticulture depends primarily upon the employees I choose, you may rest assured that I have given the subject careful thought. Almost daily, people ask me for information about how to find employment in this field. These inquiries demonstrate the need for some elementary information about this subject. The following presentation will outline the most critical points job seekers need to keep in mind.

I ask you to have patience until you discover a topic of interest, as this section has been written for an audience with varied needs and levels of experience. Therefore, not every part will have equal value or appeal for different persons. Hopefully, each reader will find in these pages some bit of information which proves helpful in landing a rewarding job in horticulture.

The first thing you should realize about horticulture is that it covers a tremendously varied subject area. Perhaps the most important contribution this book can make is to help readers become aware of the many different job opportunities which exist. Unless you have been active in horticulture for years, the numerous activities taking place in this field would probably surprise you.

Because of this diversity, it is necessary to narrow down and define our area of discussion somewhat. In this section job information which is more properly concerned with conventional agriculture or in botany will not be presented. Most dictionaries describe horticulture as dealing with the activity of growing fruits, vegetables, flowers, or ornamentals. We will discuss job opportunities in all these horticultural areas. However, the material relating to fruit and vegetable production is limited to situations in which their culture is practiced indoors or at least in very intensively managed outdoor facilities.

HORTICULTURE AN EXPANDING INDUSTRY

Every segment of horticulture has been expanding rapidly in the past several decades—a good deal faster than the general economy. The market for medicinal and edible herbs, specialty fruits and vegetables, plant related services, and other products is much greater than in the past. Ornamental horticulture, in particular, has experienced explosive growth.

The demand for ornamental plants is generated mainly by trends in national life-style which will continue unabated. Everyone is becoming more ecologically minded and more fully aware of the ethical and practical benefits which ornamental plants can add to human life and the environment. Reinforcing this change in basic national psychology is the fact that, generally, both husband and wife now work outside the home; this increases household income but reduces the time available for outdoor and indoor gardening activities.

People want to enjoy plants and flowers more but they have less time to do it. Professional horticulturists can now command an excellent income by providing the time saving goods and services which consumers demand. Ornamental horticulture is no longer an infant industry which supplies only the basics of seed, fertilizer, and perhaps a few bare root shrubs and trees; a large volume and varied assortment of sophisticated horticultural supplies and services have become more or less necessities of life to many people.

ROOM FOR INDIVIDUALS IN HORTICULTURE

Fortunately for individual job seekers and entrepreneurs, relatively little of the horticultural production industry has been invaded by large corporations. Only in the area of hard goods (such as fertilizer and pots) have they made significant inroads. Anywhere there is money to be made we can expect corporate management to investigate the possibilities. However, the inherent variability of plants, their need for constant care, and the diversity of environments in which they are utilized is not the ideal situation for the standardized methods which megabusiness is best at.

Large national corporations have tried to enter the plant growing segment of horticulture but have, in general, pulled back out as they find that producing living organisms is more complicated than manufacturing stoves and refrigerators. By far, the greatest total number of greenhouses, nurseries, and specialty production facilities throughout the United States are small to medium size and are owned by individuals who sell a good deal of their product through their own retail outlets. Even the larger production facilities are most frequently owned by individuals or closely held companies.

Marketing of greenhouse and nursery crops was formerly accomplished almost entirely through the producer's own retail facility or through numerous independent florists and garden stores. At present, a large part of ornamental plant products are sold by chain, discount, and food stores. Hardware and department stores also do a significant amount of business.

For live plants and cut flowers as a whole, perhaps a little less than half are now sold through the nontraditional outlets; of course this figure will vary greatly depending upon the exact nature of the product, geography, and demographic factors. Twenty or thirty years ago, independent operations were caught unprepared to market effectively against chain type competition. At present, however, the independents seem to have adapted well and may even be benefiting from the wide and constant public exposure which flowers and plants receive in mass outlets.

Those independent retailers who have placed their emphasis upon service, high quality, and new or unusual products seem to flourish now, while the ones who tried to compete head on in price terms with mass outlets have fallen by the wayside. Many growers of ornamentals have seized the opportunity to supply chain type outlets.

Of course, these growers must adapt to the mass market philosophy of high volume and generally lower prices for the product. Often times in this situation quality has suffered. Chains pressure the grower for lower and lower prices until factors essential for proper plant growth are sacrificed. Fortunately, most people in the industry have begun to realize the folly of this situation, and, in general, chain buyers are stressing quality more than in the past.

We may summarize the general situation in ornamental horticulture by saying that it is an industry whose exceptional growth is due to fundamental and continuing changes in national psychology and living patterns. Individuals and small companies dominate the plant growing segment, while activity in the marketing phase is split fairly evenly between chain outlets and independent operators. Although plants and flowers are often distributed nationally, market prices are still determined primarily by local factors and participants are more-or-less able to fix their own prices by providing differing levels of quality, service, and selection.

The healthy financial stature of the industry, in combination with an interesting mix of larger and smaller companies doing new things to promote their product, allows job seekers to choose from amongst numerous opportunities. Fortunately for the job applicant in horticulture, most companies in the industry still maintain a down to earth management style that does not reflect a set of rigid rules and regulations characteristic of larger corporations.

This informal atmosphere makes it easier for individuals to find and win positions which are well suited to their talents and needs. Although the owners and managers who do the hiring are concerned about productivity and profits, they are generally in very close contact with employees and understanding of their needs.

Most managers are easy to approach for a job and willing to give almost anyone a chance even if the applicant may lack some aspects of formal education or experience.

Although the horticultural industry is rather conservative in many respects, it is not a moldy group of good-old-boys who wish to keep everything the way it has been for years. For the most part, the industry is directed by practical people who get the job done by old-fashioned hard work and ingenuity, while possessing an inborn appreciation of new plant varieties and cultural methods.

Employers have little tolerance for people who wish to dabble in horticulture without doing the necessary dirty work. But dedicated "eccentrics" are accepted everywhere in this field as one of the benefits of membership in our community of plant lovers. The horticultural industry is proud of its unconventional putterers and creative designers, much as the English public is of their beloved street-corner-orators.

Horticulturists are, in general, a sensible lot of independent-minded people who are friendly but intolerant of shoddy work. And while they appreciate time for dreaming about the glories of plants, they understand the need for timely planning and execution of necessary tasks. How else could it be if one's teacher is Mother Nature? She is beautiful but unforgiving.

BASIC ORGANIZATIONAL PATTERNS IN HORTICULTURAL SPECIALTIES

If you carefully recollected the specific activity or combination of activities of each horticultural business you have visited over the years and classified these memories into logical order, you would recognize an organizational pattern similar to the one which will soon be outlined. In the process you would, of course, find that there are many hybrid operations which do not fall neatly into any one area of activity. Although each particular horticultural specialty area will be explored in more detail later, readers may benefit from having a concise preview of the industry right from the start. Some knowledge of how business is organized cannot but help when a person is searching for a job.

Production

The production phase of horticultural specialty crops is a rather obvious aspect of the industry. It is probable, however, that only a few readers have observed firsthand the actual workings of such a growing facility. Your closest experience with production operations most likely would be with a small, neighborhood greenhouse or nursery which was growing a portion of its merchandise needs while buying the rest from wholesale specialists. You are not likely to have visited the production locations of larger independent retailers or wholesale growers. Generally, the managers of these larger production operations must, out of necessity, limit the number of visitors so that work may continue without interruption.

Production facilities for horticultural specialty crops are as diverse as the particular needs of each crop and of the individuals growing it. There are different ways to solve cultural requirements and the chosen solution may vary with the materials available, climate, financing, individual inclination, and marketing objectives. The atmosphere at a production facility may range from one of complete dependence upon technical methods, to the opposite attitude where success or failure depends upon vague "feelings" the grower may have about the needs of crops. Fortunately, most modern growers lean towards the first alternative as they become aware of the competitive advantages offered by efficient, reliable crop production methods.

The size of production facilities in specialized horticultural crops ranges from tiny backyard setups, to gigantic operations. Most fall into the small or medium size range. There has been some tendency of late (particularly in the greenhouse field) for firms to expand quickly. This is only natural when growers see attractive markets without an adequate supply of products. But many growers have found that bigness does not necessarily lead to greater profits and stability. Now some growers are beginning to question the wisdom of extremely rapid growth and are concentrating more upon profitability rather than volume.

The primary driving forces for change in the production aspects of horticultural speciality crops are the decrease in availability of cheap labor and the virtual explosion in technological knowledge which is taking place. Any present day grower who does not take advantage of labor saving techniques and who does not keep abreast of new knowledge in the field will soon find that it is impossible to compete with more progressive operations.

It is absolutely essential for growers to keep themselves informed about all aspects of the industry so that they may organize their production towards the most efficient use of resources.

Marketing

The important point to be made about marketing in horticultural speciality crops is that, luckily, it generally lacks a centralized character. Centralized marketing (whether it results from government, industry, or financial interests) always tends to limit the ability of individuals to determine and ask for the price they feel is proper for their merchandise. Centralized markets (such as auctions and government and industry sponsored marketing authorities) represent an easy means for growers to sell crops. But the passive acceptance of whatever price marketing organizations allow does not usually lead to the highest possible profits for better growers. Centralized markets function best when a product possesses relatively uniform characteristics. If growers must tailor their produce to meet these uniform standards, then there is little room left for individuals who wish to distinguish their product in the public eye. This is the primary reason why mainstream food and fiber farmers have generally realized low profit levels from their operations. Within the different classes of ordinary corn which have been established by market authorities, each farmer in a region receives basically the same price at any given time. There is little incentive for product differentiation under these conditions; in fact, there is a bias against any variation.

A similar situation exists for most major commodity crops. So, while centralized marketing may function as a lubricant to effective national trading and distribution, it rarely benefits innovative growers who wish to offer products which differ from the standard version.

Since crop marketing is the most difficult part of my job, it would be nice if this task could be left to someone else. However, when the yearly accounting of profits is done, I give thanks that conscientious and knowledgeable growers like myself are able to ask for and receive prices which are much higher than the ordinary. Creating profitable market channels through active participation in the selling process is absolutely essential. It takes time, thought, and advance planning, but it is well worth the trouble. Growing plants is fun, but it soon becomes stale when monetary rewards are slim or nonexistent.

The essential points about where and by whom most horticultural speciality crops are sold have been mentioned. It is obvious that the market for these crops is evolving a two-tier structure. At the bottom are the mass outlets who deal primarily in products which are treated more-or-less as commodities; that is, those which are sold in volume, those which exhibit some degree of uniformity within classes and can be easily handled and priced, and those which require a minimum of service. On the second tier are the independent outlets which deal in more than strictly the commonplace plants and products and which offer a maximum of service. This two-tier merchandising system is evolving because of natural forces in the market place. Please recognize the reality of the situation and decide which segment is more to your taste for employment.

Services

If you pause and imagine various businesses which have some connection to horticulture, you will find that some of them offer very little in the way of tangible plant products; they sell a service, such as landscape design, plant care, or pest control. These are the more obvious aspects of service in the industry, but there is some degree of service offered with almost every plant sale. Even the least service-oriented mass outlets provide care tags with plants to help customers enjoy their purchase. And at the other end of the spectrum, the retail price of plants and flowers at some upscale specialty shops is mainly dictated by the amount of special service connected with the purchase. Some outlets for horticultural products do not have a clear vision of the relationship which connects products and services. They do not know what they are selling. This type of confused situation can lead to disastrous consequences through not pricing merchandise to include the cost of services rendered, aiming products at the wrong economic class of purchasers, and many more merchandising mistakes. Smart marketers learn to evaluate service factors correctly and how to best use them to advantage in particular business situations.

In the future, the marketing of horticultural products by independent operators will increasingly be dominated by those who are devising creative ways to provide needed services along with the plant products they wish to sell. The days when a grower could simply offer Marigold and Petunia seedlings or bare root nursery stock and expect consumers to knock down the door are over. Customers desire and need added services to satisfy new lifestyles. They will go someplace else if you don't provide what they want.

For the reasons above, the service area of horticulture offers particularly fertile ground for those people who seek employment in a challenging field with few established rules. The "sky is the limit" for creative people who are able to come up with concepts which find public acceptance and therefore sell more products.

There is a rather distinct segment of horticultural services which merits some special mention. It is the area of informational and technical and scientific services. Many consumers and perhaps even some avid horticulturists may seldom think of this as being a real part of horticulture. But it is truly the power and motivator behind improvement in the entire industry.

Although many readers may never have thought of employment in this last mentioned field, I can testify (from personal experience) that it is very rewarding both in monetary and creative satisfaction. Writers, teachers, scientists, technicians, and publishers may seldom have direct contact with the horticultural marketplace, but they provide the information necessary for smooth and profitable functioning of the industry.

TYPES OF EMPLOYMENT AVAILABLE IN HORTICULTURE

Every field of endeavor has at least several general job specialty areas. Horticulture approaches the unique because it has employment niches running the gamut from unskilled field workers through highly trained research scientists. There are outdoor jobs, indoor jobs, creative jobs, repetitive jobs—you name it and horticulture has it.

If you love plants it is likely you can find a job in horticulture that fits your skills, needs, and aspirations. But you won't find the right job unless you know what is available—that's what this section is about.

My main emphasis will be to discuss employment opportunities available in what we would term entry level jobs through middle level positions. Some mention will be made of top management positions and of those which generally require a technical education. But, obviously, these managers and college educated people are not the ones who require the most help to find a good job— hopefully they have already learned a good deal of what I shall soon present about specific job areas. This doesn't mean these people cannot benefit from reading this book— they will surely pick up a few new facts, and perhaps their thinking about employment opportunities may become more organized than it previously was.

SUGGESTED METHOD OF STUDY

Before proceeding further, take a few minutes to ponder the question, "Why am I reading this information?" Obviously, you must feel that this book may help you find something you are looking for. In other words, you hope to find an occupation which coincides with your needs, hopes, preferences, and abilities: a good job that gives you a sense of accomplishment and makes you happy.

In order to find employment of this sort you must determine just what it is you need, what your preferences are, what you hope to accomplish, and what your abilities are. It sounds simple, but, unfortunately, finding out this information is often the most difficult part of job seeking.

Begin thinking of these things in a general way right now, then turn the page and quickly study the remaining information. Don't try to figure out details as you speed along, and, above all, don't attempt to make any decisions.

Finish your first reading of this section in one sitting if you possibly can. Then let the information "stew" in your head for a few days before you pick up the book to begin a detailed study of each employment topic. Only at the end of your second reading should you feel qualified to begin making decisions about what job you want and how to go about getting it.

This two-stage method of inquiry makes my own study efforts more enjoyable and usually leads to better decisions with less difficulty.

Chapter 2

SPECIFIC EMPLOYMENT OPPORTUNITIES IN HORTICULTURE

The following discussion of specific employment areas in horticulture is arranged into groups of related opportunities. You will notice that, broadly speaking, jobs may be categorized as production, marketing, or service-oriented. However, some positions are of such a varied nature that it is difficult to pigeon hole them so neatly. Please remember that the group headings are used here primarily to facilitate discussion; they do not imply any rigid hierarchy within the industry.

Almost every horticultural endeavor is regulated to a greater-or-lesser degree by the growth and development cycles of plants or by the seasonal nature of society's demand for various plant products. Therefore, employment activity in horticulture shows exaggerated peaks and valleys not usually associated with other industries.

The spring season causes a great general high point of employment opportunity in horticulture, while other individual holidays may bring about rushes of activity within specific areas of the industry. Job seekers must examine the exact seasonal tendencies within the areas they are most interested. In so doing, their efforts at locating employment will not be wasted during inappropriate times of the year.

There are a few areas of the horticultural industry which exhibit practically no seasonal employment peaks. This scenario might be encountered in such fields as therapy, research, or publishing.

HOW MUCH CAN YOU EXPECT TO BE PAID?

It is difficult to quote definite wage guidelines within the horticultural industry. So much depends upon the nature of the job, geographic location, experience of the applicant, and many other factors. However, some general pay scales which are based mainly upon personal observation will be pointed out—remember, a specific situation could change the figures dramatically!

The 1999 wages reported here represent only what might reasonably be expected: I do not wish to paint an overly optimistic general picture and thereby give readers higher expectations than actually exist. Since these quotes are rather conservative, most variation from them would be towards an increased wage scale. Higher pay might be expected when the economy is expanding quickly, when employers are looking for especially qualified help, in certain high wage geographic regions, or for a number of other particular reasons.

Entry level horticultural jobs which require no previous training or skills would generally start at the

federally mandated minimum wage of $5.15 per hour—
this is for geographic areas where overall compensation
levels are in the lower end. In high cost of living areas,
these low skill entry-level positions might pay $1 or $2
more per hour. If heavy physical labor is required, even
entry-level wages may be $8-$12 per hour.

When the job description calls for at least a minimum
of previous experience or training, one might expect to
earn $6-$8 an hour in low cost of living areas, or perhaps
$8-$11 per hour in higher cost of living areas. Again, any
job requiring heavy physical labor or operation of
equipment would likely pay a bit more.

As we move into employment opportunities which
require a moderate to high level of skill or training, it is
more difficult to quote general wage scales. A range of
$25,000 to $50,000 per year would likely be encountered.
A premium for heavy physical labor would not often exist
here, since most of these jobs are not of the heavy labor
type. Some skilled equipment operators might also fall into
this salary bracket.

Recent college graduates with degrees appropriate to
the job description could also expect to receive offers of
$25,000 to $50,000 per year—most likely in the lower areas
of that range unless exceptional circumstances prevailed.

It should be stressed that skill or training as mentioned
here does not automatically mean formal education;
generally, it relates to previous job experience either in the
field of horticulture or a related industry.

Highly skilled positions in horticulture normally start
at over $30,000 per year and, in most cases, at over $40,000
per year. In this wage category, there is much variation,
but seldom have I observed anyone being paid over

$100,000 per year unless they own a private business. Most job seekers in the highly skilled levels are expected to have a university degree.

The salary levels mentioned here fairly well mirror compensation in other American industries. There are certain exceptions which should be noted: highly skilled horticultural workers seldom approach the salary levels of certain high paying professions—such as medical doctors and lawyers. And there is only minor union activity in horticulture—this means there are few jobs in horticulture comparable to the factory jobs available in autos, steel, aerospace, etc.

Job related benefits in horticulture also mirror the American workplace. If any generality can be made, benefits may sometimes be lower in horticulture because of the reduced union activity mentioned above. Any future federally mandated medical insurance programs would likely improve the benefit picture in horticulture relative to union factories and service industries.

The strongest points which can be made for horticulture as a career are:

- The healthy financial condition of the industry as a whole—it is expanding rapidly.
- The tremendous number of personally fulfilling jobs which are available—horticulture is a happy industry overall when compared to other dreary prospects.
- Horticulture generally provides a healthful workplace—many jobs offer a pleasant mix of indoor and outdoor work.

Readers must not expect that every detail about finding a good job in horticulture will be spelled out in the following pages. The presentation is meant to guide you in the right direction, but it cannot cover all the variations in employment which may occur due to local geography, business conditions, climate, labor availability, and a hundred other possible factors.

Therefore, the main responsibility for finding the best job rests with you. Use the guidelines presented here, but make sure you adequately research the local scene. If your investigation seems to contradict information given here, check it out again and then go with your best judgement rather than blindly accepting my assessment of the situation. After all, there is no way I can be aware of the exact conditions prevailing in every American community.

A good job working with plants, trees, and flowers will not materialize out of thin air. You must look for it conscientiously. And don't always expect your efforts to take effect immediately; sometimes it requires considerable work to find exactly what you are seeking. If you demonstrate energy, persistence and organization, your search for a job will be rewarded.

EMPLOYMENT IN PLANT GROWING FACILITIES—COMMERCIAL

Our discussion of specific jobs in horticulture will begin by acquainting you with those areas where the chief duties are actually concerned with growing plants in some capacity or another.

Many horticultural crops are grown indoors under the protection of some type of structure. Although the construction of such indoor facilities may vary considerably, the common name generally given to all of them is "greenhouse."

Another large group of crops, such as trees and shrubs, are traditionally grown outdoors in very intensely managed fields or nursery grounds. There are some situations where it is difficult to classify culture as indoor or outdoor—such might be the case when shade houses are widely employed or when other temporary protective shelters are provided for crops.

Although particular crops are grown most frequently in one of these types of cultural settings or the other, special circumstances may warrant growing certain plants in both indoor and outdoor environments.

As an example (in most regions), potted flowers generally are grown in greenhouses, but producers in Florida and California frequently grow certain varieties outdoors during warmer seasons. Another example: both ornamental and reforestation trees are typically grown outdoors after they are well-established, but many often spend the early part of their life in climate controlled greenhouses.

As time passes, it is becoming more common to grow a larger proportion of crops for a longer period of time under some type of controlled environment. The object being to exert closer control over all factors which affect the growth, marketability, and profitability of plants. Owners have a desire to produce crops not only as inexpensively as possible, but also in a predictable fashion. In many cases, the most profitable long term method of operation is to bring crops under protection.

The tendency towards greater control over crops has caused a good deal of change in the types and numbers of jobs available in horticultural plant production. There is now a higher proportion of jobs in the technical area than previously existed. And less jobs, proportionately, in manual labor or unskilled positions.

When "technical area" is mentioned, most readers may think of "growers" who manage the cultural requirements of plants. But there are other technical positions available in growing operations—particularly in the larger facilities. Most good size greenhouses and nurseries will have an equipment and structure technician whose duty it is to make sure all the various machines and buildings used in production work smoothly and efficiently.

Some production companies may have full or part time sales persons and transportation people to market crops. There are many other possible jobs in greenhouses and nurseries: in the office or laboratory, in accounting, truck drivers, custodial help, etc.

Obviously, there is no place in this book to describe all these support positions—we must limit our discussion to a few important (and plant related) employment opportunities.

Horticultural crop production facilities range in size from tiny one person operations to mammoth companies that grow and market on a global scale. Most facilities are of small to medium size and one person may take care of several areas of responsibility. Thus, the grower in a small nursery may also take care of the machinery and handle marketing and business finances. In a large production facility, different individuals would most likely be responsible for each area. The largest companies may have many growers.

Growers

In the modern world, professional plant growing is a highly technical field. It is true that many "old time" growers and "hit or miss" amateur growers are still active in commercial horticulture, but intense competition now dictates that crops be grown precisely and as inexpensively as possible by trained professionals.

In order to become a good grower, one must acquire the necessary expertise through job experience or through formal educational programs. The best growers have participated in both types of training. It is very difficult to learn everything in the classroom or through books, and it is equally impossible to truly understand the complexities of plant production when on the job experience is the only learning tool available.

The traditional method of becoming a grower was to follow an apprentice program of one type or another. A person would start with a nursery or greenhouse as an unskilled worker, then graduate to assistant grower, and finally to grower. Eventually, they might become head grower if the firm employed several.

For most small horticultural production companies, on the job experience is still the primary route to a grower job.

A university degree in horticulture is normally required by larger production facilities as a condition of employment. With additional on the job experience, the graduate will progress to head grower or production manager.

There is a great need for alternative means of training horticultural growers. The apprentice system is outdated in many respects, and university programs are simply too expensive and time consuming. Some community colleges and technical schools are beginning to fill the need for a middle ground, but these programs are few and far between.

Readers who wish to become commercial growers must plan ahead to acquire the necessary skills; a horticultural producer would seldom hire a grower who lacked commercial experience in the field. Even university graduates in horticulture might receive few job offers if they had not worked in greenhouses, nurseries, or other operations for at least a few months prior to receiving a degree.

Growing plants commercially is totally different than puttering with them on an amateur basis. Don't think that you can be a successful commercial grower just because you are an excellent gardener. It is true that both pursuits require a person to love plants and have some sort of "feel" for a plant's needs. But the commercial grower must also be technically-oriented, well-organized, aware of marketing conditions, and able to manage helpers efficiently. The best growers are part artist, part business person, and part scientist. In most situations, they must also lend a hand in the day to day work of the operation.

Obviously, not all grower jobs are the same. The nature of responsibilities will vary for many reasons. But the size of the operation a person is working for is a major determinant of job characteristics. Larger production facilities almost always require a grower to be more technically proficient and organized. You must decide what type of grower position you will be capable of filling and which type will make you happiest. Then aim your training and job seeking efforts at that type of position.

No matter what type of grower position you wish to acquire, some practical experience in production facilities is going to be the most helpful prerequisite. The easiest way to get that experience is to hire on as an unskilled worker at a nursery, greenhouse, or other production facility. These types of jobs are much more numerous than are grower positions and offer you an easy means of getting a foot in the door.

I have not spoken at any length about the actual job functions of a grower—the general thrust of the work should be obvious from the title. Any further detail would require many hours of your time to adequately address the subject. Readers who wish to find out about the type of knowledge a modern grower must possess can get a good idea by reading *The Greenhouse And Nursery Handbook*. Admittedly, this book covers only the fields mentioned in the title, but much of the technical knowledge is similar for any specialty area.

The job of being a grower is very rewarding if you are a plant lover. Every horticulturist knows the special feeling a person experiences when working amongst beautifully grown plants. But the job can also be nerve racking when unforeseen calamities threaten crop failure. You must be prepared for either situation.

Non-technical growing jobs

The great majority of positions available at horticultural production facilities fall into this category. In these jobs, people are working directly with plants most of the time, but they are not responsible (as is the grower) for scheduling or determining cultural programs for the crops.

Many facilities label these non-technical production people as assistant growers if they have been hired as trainees who aspire to become growers. Most recently hired production workers are not given any special title. They are simply hired to get a job done, and any future progress by them usually comes about because of the initiative and capability which they show on the job.

Unless you have some specific desirable horticultural training or talent, you would very likely start work in a production facility as an entry level worker. Although the pay scale and responsibility level enjoyed at this position may not meet your eventual expectations, there are excellent prospects for quick advancement for anyone who displays desirable work habits and intelligence.

Even in modern mechanized production operations, there is still a great amount of hand labor involved. Numerous seasonal workers are usually hired, and they need supervision. If you have the ability and taste for supervising other people, chances are that your talents could be quickly put to use in this type of situation. Since numerous entry level jobs are filled by seasonal migrants or recent immigrants from Mexico, a speaking knowledge of Spanish is often a valuable skill to possess. In fact, if you are a Latino who knows a little about any aspect of horticulture, your language capabilities could help you land a management position.

The great need for seasonal workers provides opportunity for almost anyone to get a job in horticultural production at the entry level. But once your foot is in the door, it is then up to you to use the position as a stepping stone to better and longer term opportunities.

There are a large number of horticulturally inclined people who prefer to work only on a seasonal basis. For one reason or another, a year-round job does not fit their plans. Plenty of work exists at plant production facilities for people like this, especially in the spring. However, you may find it difficult to advance very far professionally if you only work part of the year.

Many greenhouses and nurseries hire the same local people year after year for seasonal work—and in some cases, these persons may supervise crews of less experienced temporary workers. This is a case where some upward mobility is possible for part time employees. Good permanent jobs may not open up every year at a particular facility, but when one does it is often filled by a seasonal employee who has come back for 2 or 3 seasons.

A non-technical growing job can be very pleasant employment. You are working directly with the plants, and, yet, you are not usually responsible for the nerve racking mental decisions which the professional grower must make. For some people this is exactly the position they prefer, though the pay may be limited.

Certain entry level growing jobs can be physically demanding—especially those which require outdoor work during all types of weather and those where the plants being handled are large and heavy (a tree nursery for example). If you are not up to this type of exertion, be sure you mention the fact at your first interview. I have personally seen several people reach the exhaustion point as they worked at tasks which they simply could not handle but were too proud to quit once they had started.

The actual tasks which are performed in non-technical growing jobs are quite varied, depending mostly upon the type of crop being grown. The degree of modern advancement and the physical size of facilities are also major influencing factors. Almost every crop requires the same basic care. Plants must be planted, transported, watered, fertilized, pruned, and harvested. Each crop may need a special variation in treatment, but 90% of the growing work done in a production facility revolves around these half-dozen essentials.

Some operations are quite modern so that a great deal of the actual work is performed by machines. People are present only to monitor the machines and perform tasks that are not possible to complete mechanically. Other growing operations have only a minimum of mechanization and require a large number of people to perform the same tasks day after day. Each type of operation can be profitable, and each can be rewarding to work in—it depends upon your preferences. Mechanized facilities usually pay entry level people at a better rate than do those that are less mechanized.

Structural and mechanical technician

Larger plant production operations accumulate a good deal of machinery and, depending upon the type of crops grown, may have an extensive array of buildings. Both of which require regular upkeep in order to function dependably. Greenhouse ranges especially need constant supervision to prevent interruption of essential crop services. Heating, irrigation, and ventilation systems are the primary concerns along with general structural repair.

In most cases the facility will have "in house" technicians to take care of all but the most extensive mechanical and structural repair and installation. Most of these people function primarily as "handymen," but at least the supervisors must possess special skills in order to handle the more complex problems which arise and to monitor the overall operation.

Mechanical and structural technicians may be chosen from among seasonal crop workers, or they may be hired specifically for their appropriate skills. Carpentry, plumbing, electrical, and automotive skills are valuable around a greenhouse or nursery—there is always something to be installed, adjusted, or repaired.

The supervisor of this work category has considerable responsibility since a breakdown in essential services can be catastrophic to the operation.

Persons wishing to work in the mechanical and structural positions should expect at least some heavy and dirty work on different construction and repair projects.

Salesperson

Small greenhouses, nurseries, and other crop facilities seldom employ a designated salesperson, but larger operations often have at least one individual who spends most of his or her time on marketing efforts.

While some horticulturists might shudder at the thought of selling plants, this work is essential to the continued existence of any growing operation, and, if you possess the proper temperament, it can be a lot of fun. The exact duties of this job can vary considerably depending upon the type of operation and its marketing program.

There are lots of differences between selling retail as opposed to wholesale, but every salesperson must be persistent, believe in their product, and like to meet people.

Many horticultural producers fail to recognize how extremely important it is to have well-trained people executing the marketing program. This is a shame because most business failures in the industry arise not because of poor growing practices, but rather from weak marketing abilities.

The sales job often falls by default upon a secretary or other office person who is nearest the telephone. This is all wrong! Salespersons should be carefully chosen for their ability to communicate with people, and they should be given adequate instructions about the product they are expected to sell.

I have often heard people describe another person as "a born salesman." This statement holds a good deal of truth. In my experience it is much easier to make an excellent salesperson out of someone who has the natural talent but may possess little technical knowledge of the product than to do the opposite.

Although you may land a horticultural sales job by applying for that particular position, the ultimate goal might be more easily reached in most cases by going to work at one of the numerous entry level growing jobs or in the general office staff. After gaining a toe hold, then you can assess the situation and plan your next step.

Although many owners and managers of production facilities may fail to initially realize the importance of a highly qualified salesperson, not too many of them remain in the dark for long once they experience an increase in sales and profits due to that person's efforts. Sales persons should devise some means of documenting the extra business they bring in and use this information as a measure of their progress when negotiating salary. This must be done right from the start or the boss may not understand that the improvements are due to your efforts.

The salary for a salesperson can range from one of the highest in the company to one of the lowest. Some companies realize how valuable these people are, while some do not. It is up to you to correct the error in the latter case by showing exactly what can be accomplished by a skilled and energetic sales effort. Remember, the increase in sales must be documented and proven to have occurred due to your work rather than some other cause. A word of caution should be injected here—don't step on everyone's toes by trying to show what a sales whiz you are. Present the facts, and let them speak for themselves. Supervisors may become irritated if you infer that they haven't been doing the best job in the past.

Selling horticultural products can be very rewarding. In this job you reap the benefits of all who labored before you to produce a beautiful plant. There is real joy in selling good merchandise—especially if you can get the job done with mutual benefit to each participant in the transaction.

When you are a successful salesperson, the customers you service will become your biggest fans. They will ask for you by name each time they want to do business. When this happens frequently, the owner or manager will quickly realize that you are a very important part of the operation.

Production manager & general manager

Only a few moments will be taken to describe these positions since there are obviously only limited openings each year which require such a high level of skill. In family owned operations, these positions are normally filled by a specific member of the family—at least until the firm grows to considerable size.

The production manager coordinates the business strategy formulated by the general manager with the efforts of growers and salespersons. Since horticultural products are very perishable, the production manager must possess considerable skill in juggling production with estimated sales. This is not an easy job.

The general manager is responsible for making sure that all aspects of the business function smoothly together. Development of a coherent business philosophy is the most important function of this person. Finances are often a major concern of the general manager.

Types of commercial horticultural production

The general employment opportunities within

commercial plant production operations have been described. A more complete idea of the employment possibilities may possibly be gained by listing some of the more important facets of commercial production.

The following examples could generally be either retail or wholesale businesses. Certain types of facilities, such as hydroponic greenhouses and farm crop transplant producers, are much more likely to sell on a wholesale basis, while the majority of small ornamental greenhouses and nurseries probably depend upon retail business for most of their sales.

In order to keep the discussion as short as possible, the reader will be left to individually interpret how job opportunities might be affected by the retail or wholesale emphasis of a particular production operation. The previous production job descriptions have perhaps emphasized more of a wholesale situation, while a later section dealing with retail horticultural employment will deal exclusively with retail situations.

You must be aware that thousands of production operations fall in between the two types—in fact, the intermediates may be more numerous than the extremes. In other words, many production operations sell plants or other produce at both the retail and wholesale level. Keep this in mind as you evaluate what opportunities seem most appropriate for you.

A. Greenhouses: An endless array of crops are grown in greenhouses—some for the entire production sequence and some for only a short establishment period.

• Ornamental greenhouses—Potted flowers, cut flowers, foliage plants, and spring bedding plants are the usual type of merchandise grown here. Other specialized crops, such as Bonsai trees and water garden plants, may be grown under cover. Although cut flowers were the most popular crop years ago, potted flowers and bedding plants have become the important crops at present in North America.

- Hydroponic greenhouses—Vegetables are the main crop grown here, and herbs are also becoming important. Although there are some small hydroponic growing operations, the nature of the business usually dictates that larger establishments are more likely to survive. Some types of cut flowers and other specialty crops are also grown hydroponically.
- Farm transplant greenhouses—In some sections of the country, there are extensive greenhouse ranges which produce small seedlings for use in agricultural operations. Cabbage and other cole crops, Tomatoes, Tobacco, Sugar Beets, and many other plants are often handled this way. The greenhouse is frequently owned by individual farmers, but there are some large greenhouse operations which specialize in this type of production.

B. Container tree nurseries: These nurseries are usually located outdoors but may have significant greenhouse space for younger stock. And some stock may be grown in a traditional field situation until it is containerized. Therefore, the container tree nursery is often somewhat of a hybrid operation between indoor and field culture. And it need not always grow only trees; in fact, most grow lots of shrubs and some also grow herbaceous perennials. Ornamentals are the usual crop grown here because the plants are of high enough value to warrant the expenses of planting into pots.

Some large companies have horticultural divisions which grow millions of trees for replanting logged areas, revegetating coal mines, etc. These operations are usually very modern and may or may not grow plants in containers. The trend is moving towards more production in some type of specialized container so that the survival of the transplant at remote sites is better assured.

C. Open field plant production: Almost all horticultural crops are sometimes grown in intensely managed fields in particular locations or under certain circumstances. The following is a quick listing of some more important types of operations:

- Cut flowers
- Perennial ornamentals.
- Ornamental trees and shrubs.
- Herbs, both medicinal and culinary.
- Market garden vegetables, berries, etc.
- Christmas trees, holly.
- Lawn sod and plugs.

EMPLOYMENT IN PLANT GROWING SITUATIONS—NON-COMMERCIAL

It is difficult to easily distinguish between commercial (previously discussed) and non-commercial plant growing situations. By describing an operation as a commercial producer, I mean to say that the main activity engaged in is to grow plants for eventual sale at retail or wholesale. In non-commercial, I mean to include all those situations where plants are grown for use or enjoyment on the premises or a closely adjacent property. Services for and upkeep of plants are often a major part of the employment program in non-commercial circumstances. The actual sale of plants is seldom engaged in. Display of the plants for enjoyment or other purposes is usually a frequent service objective, but there may be other objectives such as lawn use for sporting events (football, golf, etc.), research and cultural programs (arboretums and botanical gardens), or therapy (nursing homes, handicapped facilities).

Persons employed in a non-commercial growing capacity may need to possess skills not only necessary for growing plants but also for the other objectives of the particular program—display, upkeep, explanation and information about plants, preparation for research use, etc.

The following is a listing of various employment possibilities for you to consider:

- Botanic gardens and arboretums.
- City and county parks.
- Cemeteries, public schools, fairgrounds.
- Federal and state parks.
- University and college grounds.
- Private estates.
- Miscellaneous public and private facilities—sports grounds, race courses, events centers, resorts, airports, malls, amusement parks, theme parks, condominiums, golf courses, private business grounds and interiors, libraries, churches, hospitals, medical buildings, nursing homes, etc. You may undoubtedly think of several other situations where the use of plants is so extensive as to require the attention of a full or part time employee for growing, upkeep, and services.
- Private and public businesses or agencies which have considerable need for plants to conduct research or carry on business—agricultural companies, food companies, seed companies, tree companies, breweries, federal food and drug departments, federal and state agriculture departments, universities, reclamation companies, etc.

This presentation concerning employment in the plant growing areas of horticulture is too short to explain all the various possibilities available to you. But I believe the best course is to leave out excessive details, so that a clearer overall picture is readily apparent. Further discussion might confuse some readers with too many facts which are interesting but do not appreciably clarify a person's basic understanding of the field.

The next topic will deal with employment opportunities in the retail areas of horticulture. In other words, selling plants to the general public.

PLANT MARKETING EMPLOYMENT—RETAIL

A few pages back, you will remember I stressed that many plant growing establishments also sell on a retail basis. As we discuss retail-oriented employment, please keep in mind that growing and retailing are often done simultaneously at the same operation, and readers must continually be aware that a plant growing job and a selling job are not mutually exclusive. They may be combined within a single position available to individuals.

Selling plants or other horticultural merchandise to the public is a lot of fun if you like to deal with people on a daily basis, and if you are thoroughly familiar with the products being sold.

Need for horticultural training in retailing

The single greatest need in commercial horticulture today is in the area of training people to become informed and helpful sales representatives who can efficiently provide the critical link between growers and consumers. These salespersons must have both the employer's and consumer's welfare in mind as they perform their job.

Too many salespersons think that their only mission is to make the sale. But they should also be worrying about the customer's eventual satisfaction. This latter attitude is important in any business, but it is even more critical when selling plants. Repeat purchases by satisfied customers are especially important here—trust is the most valuable asset of any horticultural company.

Retail employment in horticulture is available in almost every small town in America, and there are thousands of such jobs in each large city. Finding employment is simply a matter of knowing where to look and being persistent in your efforts.

Two general categories of retail outlets

Horticultural crops are sold at the retail level by two general categories of outlets: 1) traditional independent outlets like greenhouses, nurseries, garden centers, flower shops (a few of these outlets may be associated in small chains), and 2) non-traditional outlets such as discount stores, supermarkets, hardware stores, lumber stores, etc. (most of these are associated in chains).

You can readily see that the two contrasting avenues of selling will generally have different marketing strategies. Traditional outlets usually stress a high level of service and charge moderate to high prices, while the chain stores normally focus upon low prices with minimal service. Although chain stores are making attempts to increase services to a reasonable level, they will most likely never reach a high degree of expertise in this area since this would require more expense than their low price philosophy could tolerate.

Job seekers in retail horticulture must take note of this fundamental difference between the two main marketing avenues and choose to work in the area which offers the best chance of fulfilling the applicant's needs. Both the chain type and traditional independent outlets have their good and bad points. The job seeker must evaluate these characteristics and choose between them. Some persons will be happier working at a chain store, while others may feel the traditional type outlet is best for them.

The following listing will give you some idea of the distinguishing points which commonly differentiate the two types of retail outlets.

Chain outlet

1. Service to customer minimized.
2. Growing plants seldom a part of the operation.
3. Employees seldom trained in horticulture.
4. Manager of department seldom a knowledgeable horticulturist.
5. Selection of plants and plant products usually limited to common items.
6. Low price is the chief marketing tool in most cases.
7. More emphasis on "bread and butter" items.
8. Often handles more hard goods than green goods.
9. Tend to rely upon special "sales" for moving merchandise.
10. Often handles plant varieties which are not adapted to the local climate.
11. Garden department seldom open out of season.

Independent outlet

1. Service to customer offered at a higher level.
2. Growing plants frequently a part of the operation.
3. Employees often trained in horticulture.
4. Manager of business often a knowledgeable horticulturist.
5. Selection of plants and plant products likely to be extensive.
6. Price is only one of the many marketing tools, it is seldom the major consideration.
7. Increased availability of "artistic" items.
8. Green goods are usually the main merchandise for sale.
9. More likely to limit reliance upon special "sales" to accomplish marketing objectives.
10. Seldom allows poorly adapted plant varieties to be sold.
11. Garden department often open most of the year.

After reading this list, it might seem as if consumers would be lacking in good sense if they chose to buy plants, flowers, or trees at a chain type outlet. At almost every point, the traditional independent outlet seems to provide more incentive to shop with them. Except in the critical area of price! And who can deny this is a major consideration for many customers?

The numerous favorable aspects of traditional horticultural outlets is exactly why they have not been completely eliminated in favor of chain outlets. At the present time, about 1/2 of ornamental plants, trees, and flowers are sold at traditional outlets. Although the percentage of total industry sales in these independent outlets was declining for many years, it seems to have stabilized at approximately 50% in the last 10 years.

Obviously, there are two very different segments of the retail horticultural industry in which people can choose to work. Each offers distinctive career opportunities.

Which type of retail outlet should you choose?

Most plant lovers would initially indicate a preference for working in the traditional independent horticultural outlet because there is more emphasis on plants in this setting. However, let's examine the situation more closely and see if there aren't good reasons why at least some horticulturists would be better off working in a chain outlet. The following generalizations in favor of employment at chain type outlets might be made (remember there may be significant exceptions to these observations):

- In some cases, chain type outlets have better starting wages and benefits.
- There may be more room for advancement in chains. The top positions in small family run outfits are usually filled by family members.
- If you are a well-informed horticulturist, you may find less competition for higher paying jobs at the chains (most of their employees probably lack any significant training in the field).
- Larger chain outlets are generally more financially stable than are independent outlets.
- Chain outlets are more likely to have formal guidelines concerning employee/employer relationships—this type of

structured work environment helps employees clearly understand their rights and obligations.

- If a retailing company advances to the point of having numerous stores, it probably has a successful track record. It makes sense to associate yourself with a winning team.
- Employees of chain type outlets often receive discounts on a wide variety of merchandise from the store. This can be important if daily necessities are available.
- A chain outlet may have locations all over the nation, thus providing some degree of job stability if you must relocate, or if the store you work at eliminates your position for some reason.
- If I had to make a wager as to whether chain stores or independent outlets would generally be more successful in the next 10 years, I would place my bet on the chain stores. Any new marketing developments are more likely to favor them.

Mail order—a special retailing situation

Many companies sell plants to consumers by mail order. Although the chances of one of these firms being located in your local area is not especially high, you should not ignore this possibility of employment. Study several winter issues of your favorite gardening magazines, and see if there are any advertisements from mail order companies located where you would like to work. If there are, it is a simple matter to contact the firm to inquire about a job.

These same mail order companies may also have jobs available in the plant growing operations they maintain. Ask about employment in this capacity also.

Characteristics of retail employment in horticulture

As in other aspects of horticultural employment, there is a good deal of seasonality in the retail sector. There are many permanent year-round jobs available, but they are more difficult to find. The best way to find permanent employment is to sign up for one of the easily available seasonal jobs; if you perform well, there is a good chance you will be kept on after the busy season.

Almost every retail horticultural business is *desperate* for good help during their peak selling times. Spring is the big season for most retail operations, but there may be other busy periods in certain types of stores. Christmas is a busy time for flower shops and for garden stores that handle Christmas trees or other holiday merchandise. You can probably think of several other specialized situations.

Getting a job at these times is quite easy if you contact the boss several months ahead of time to get your name on the list of prospective workers. Ask about when you should give them a return call to confirm your availability. You must maintain contact until an opening occurs; do not expect the boss to vividly remember your first inquiry. Persistence will pay off as long as you don't make a pest of yourself.

Selling plants and other horticultural merchandise is, of course, the main activity in a retail outlet. But there are other types of jobs which may be available. As an example, someone must provide care for the plants, and there may be a need to deliver them and provide installation in the customer's building or landscape.

Certain types of retail horticultural stores offer specialized services such as floral arrangements or landscape consultation. There are many positions available in specialties such as this which may or may not require participation in the actual sales transaction.

Most entry level jobs in the retail aspects of horticulture require that a variety of duties be performed by a single person. This makes life interesting and allows you to become familiar with many aspects of the company. Such experience can help you choose an area in which you may want to specialize for further advancement.

Becoming an accomplished salesperson is not an easy task; it requires a good amount of personal talent and some technical skills. Most companies realize this and are on the lookout for good people to train as sales managers. If you perform well, there is a good chance of becoming a manager even if you lack formal training. A natural inclination towards helping customers is the key ingredient in sales. You either have it or you don't. Of course that doesn't mean your talent can't be improved upon by practice, dedication, and study.

There is a lot more that could be said about employment in retail horticulture, but readers will benefit much more from a simple suggestion: Take an afternoon off and go visit the types of retail outlets I mentioned at the start of this discussion. You will be welcome at any of these establishments, and they can be found even in most small towns. I'm sure you will benefit greatly from this field trip. Even if you don't ask questions, you can learn a lot by careful observation.

PLANT MARKETING EMPLOYMENT—WHOLESALE

The ordinary person who has purchased flowers, lawn and garden plants, or other horticultural merchandise probably has at least a passing acquaintance with the most important retail marketing channels for these products. But only a few people are likely to know anything about the behind-the-scenes wholesale activity in horticulture.

We have spoken previously about salespersons who represent nurseries and greenhouses, but there are several other possible employment areas in the wholesale trade. Many national seed, plant, and nursery stock distributors have sales representatives in every part of the country. And there are an even greater number of local and regional distributors who employ sales people. Some of these distributors require a college degree (hopefully in horticulture or a related field) as a condition of employment, but a significant number will hire people who have some practical horticultural or sales experience.

Distributors and manufacturers of equipment, structures, fertilizers, plant containers, etc. also maintain extensive sales forces. You would be surprised at the thousands of products which are essential to the horticultural industry. Someone has to sell all of them.

Most large cities have wholesale markets for cut flowers and other fresh horticultural produce. There are a few cities which also have wholesale markets for potted flowers, indoor foliage plants, and fresh Christmas items. Even medium size cities will usually have a wholesale house which distributes horticultural hard goods to local stores.

In order to find the better jobs in national or regional wholesale firms, it is often necessary to look for employment offerings in the classified section of regional or national trade magazines. Occasionally you will also notice other horticultural jobs in your locality listed within these magazines; especially if it is a regional publication. I will mention how to locate trade magazines in a later discussion.

SERVICE-ORIENTED EMPLOYMENT

There is no easy definition of exactly what a horticultural service company does. Basically, it emphasizes providing services such as landscaping or lawn care to a greater extent than it does selling plants or other physical products. There may be retail outlets that offer lots of services in addition to merchandise, and there may be service firms which sell a good deal of actual products. These hybrid operations are very common.

Service companies usually have two types of jobs available: 1) those that deal with the technical aspects of marketing of services, and 2) those that are concerned primarily with providing the actual service. The first types of positions will usually require some expertise in the particular service area, while those jobs where the actual service labor is provided will generally not require experience (except for supervising personnel).

In addition to lawn care and outdoor landscaping, there are horticultural service jobs available in interior design and landscape, tree pruning, pest control, plant rental and plant care. There are numerous jobs available everywhere in outdoor landscaping, lawn care, and tree care, but most of these positions are temporary, and many of them require heavy physical labor.

EMPLOYMENT IN HORTICULTURAL INFORMATION SERVICES

Not many readers are likely to be familiar with possible jobs in what I term the informational area of horticulture. Although positions here are not numerous in comparison to other categories, they are significant and often offer good wages for rather pleasant work.

Included here is employment by newspapers, magazines, newsletters, radio, television, plant associations and organizations, schools, colleges, trade schools, etc. In other words, any position where horticultural information is the chief product. All these garden columns, magazine articles, and television shows must be generated by people who know something about plants.

Employment in the information area may represent a regular job, or it may often be paid for on the basis of specific projects completed (such as magazine articles published). Most positions will require a good deal of expertise in the subject area. After all, if you are teaching horticulture at night school, you must know more than the students. Much of my own work in horticulture has consisted of providing information to people.

SCIENTIFIC AND TECHNICAL EMPLOYMENT

There are thousands of good paying positions all over the country in this area. Although most of these positions will require a university degree in some area of plant science, people who have other scientific degrees or at least a good deal of practical experience in the technical aspects of horticulture may qualify.

It is surprising how many private companies, grower organizations, colleges, federal and state departments, reclamation companies, and environmental organizations have a need for people with technical knowledge of plants or of factors which affect plant life.

You never know where these types of positions might turn up. When I graduated from college, I was surprised to receive a job inquiry from a soup company. After a bit of investigation, the offer didn't seem so strange because soup companies are heavily dependent upon vegetable production and processing.

The school you received a degree at can often provide help in reaching some of these employers, but most of the work is up to you. A good deal of research is necessary to identify possible employers, and further work is required to contact them.

If you are interested in foreign employment, there may be a place for your skills in the Peace Corps. This organization has many plant related openings. Call 1-800-424-8580, or check the phone book under U.S. Government for a recruiting office near you.

EMPLOYMENT IN HORTICULTURAL THERAPY

This is a field which few people know about, and, I must confess, my own knowledge is rather meager. It is my personal opinion that horticultural therapy could become a very important job market for the horticultural industry in future years.

The therapeutic value of working with plants has been recognized for many years, but it is only recently that the field has received some of the recognition it deserves from mainstream treatment providers such as doctors, hospitals, and nursing facilities. Along with recognition also comes funding.

A publication by the American Horticultural Association, which will be mentioned in the next chapter, has a good deal of information about how to reach numerous horticultural therapy associations. This would be a good place to begin your search for job opportunities in this field. You can also contact obvious local facilities which might have employment available in some aspect of horticultural therapy. Hospitals, nursing homes, Veteran's hospitals, psychiatric facilities, and community organizations for the handicapped are a few logical places to look. Positions in therapy may require technical training in this specialty or perhaps only in general horticultural skills.

Chapter 3

HOW TO GET THE JOB YOU WANT

The job you want will not be offered out of the blue; you must look for it, and you must win it. Don't expect to call one prospective employer on the phone and be hired immediately. Your search will take some time and advance planning if you are to land a desirable position.

The suggestions offered in this chapter will hopefully make your job hunting progress more quickly and smoothly. First, you will be given some ideas about where to start looking for specific job openings and then some pointers about how to prepare for and how to conduct yourself during the job interview. You have most likely been previously exposed to these job interview suggestions, but a quick summary of them can do no harm.

FIND OUT WHERE THE JOBS ARE

Pointing out the exact place you should look for a job in each horticultural specialty area is clearly beyond the scope of this book. But I can suggest some helpful starting points which will lead you to specific employment offerings.

Some types of horticultural job offerings are easy to locate, while others in more specialized areas of interest require considerable research to find. You must be persistent and thorough when searching for job openings; after all, the more employment offers you investigate, the more likely you are to find just the right job at a favorable pay scale.

Another consideration which you should keep in mind is that many horticultural jobs are offered at specific times of the year. Mid-to-late winter is often the best time to begin looking for employment in greenhouses, nurseries, and many other specialty areas which require extra help for the spring season. This is not to say that you should limit your search to the peak employment seasons, but you are more likely to be successful at that time.

Each specialty area generally has its own busy season. Jobs in lawn care are obviously more abundant in the summer, but this is the worst time to look for employment in flower shops (they do the most business from Thanksgiving through Mother's Day). Evaluate each specialty area you are interested in and try to determine the best time period in which to concentrate your search.

It is generally best to make job inquiries about 2-4 weeks before you think the employer will need someone. Applying somewhat earlier is safer, but you will need to make contact again at a later date to make sure they still remember your interest. If you do not know when the proper time to apply for jobs is, ask 2 or 3 prospective employers in that specialty area. They will be happy to advise you if you don't make a pest of yourself by hanging around too long at a time when they have no immediate need of your services.

Some horticultural specialty areas do not have a particular time of year when it is best to look for jobs. Positions in such fields as research, magazine writing, and therapy are not likely to be offered more at one time than another.

Let's now examine some of the sources you might use to find listings for specific jobs. Certain of these sources will be obvious to many readers, but each of you will probably find at least 1 or 2 new ideas here.

- **Telephone book Yellow Pages**—This is the most useful job hunting tool available. Study the Yellow Pages carefully, and make a list of all the prospective employers that were mentioned in the last chapter. If you do a good job of this, you will probably amass a considerable list of businesses which obviously have some connection to horticulture.

    Certain businesses or other types of employers may have horticultural jobs available, though they have no obvious connection to the field. For example: large shopping malls often have a person in charge of their interior plant decor and another person to take care of the outdoor landscape plantings. Several assistant positions may also be available.

    Don't forget to look for probable employers in the Yellow Pages of surrounding towns. And, if you are willing to relocate, larger cities will have an even greater number of opportunities.

- **State and private employment offices**—This is not the best place to find a job, but it is worth keeping your name in their files. Although most horticultural employers do not list their openings with general employment agencies, there are a significant number who do. If you will be satisfied with a seasonal or more generalized horticultural job, the employment office may work well for you. But specialized positions seldom turn up here.

- **Special horticultural employment agencies**—Although
regular employment agencies are often of little value in finding
specialized positions, there are several horticulturally-oriented
employment agencies which operate more or less on a
nationwide basis. These agencies advertise in a few select
magazines which appeal to avid amateur horticulturists and
to professionals in the field. Don't expect to see their
advertisements in ordinary gardening magazines. You will
sometimes find them in the classified section of *Horticulture*
and other upscale publications.

   Horticulturally-oriented employment agencies often place
classified advertisements in professional industry magazines
(those relating to greenhouses, nurseries, vegetable
production, hydroponic growing, floral marketing and
production, interior and exterior landscaping, etc.). In a few
moments, I will show you how to locate these magazines.

   Horticultural employment agencies specialize primarily in
management and technical jobs. This is one of the best ways
to look for a position if you are willing to relocate and if you
have a reasonable level of experience or a college degree in
some field.

   In most cases, this service costs you nothing because the
employment agency gets paid by the employer. The agency
seldom advertises specific jobs; you must contact them to
receive a rundown on what positions they have available.
Agencies normally do not handle temporary positions or the
more common locally available jobs. They may sometimes
have entry level positions for technical and management
specialties.

- **Professional industry magazines**—Almost every
horticultural specialty is represented by some type of
publication. Your problem is to find the specific magazines
and see if there are job listings in them. Frankly, I am not
aware of every magazine in horticulture and related fields—
so I can't provide a complete list of them. But there is a
considerable list provided in the ending resource section of
this book.

The best way to find and contact any periodical for any imaginable subject is to go to your local library and ask the librarian to show you where their reference books which list periodicals are located. They should have at least one set of the more widely used references. If you can't figure out how to use the reference book, ask the librarian for help.

Most references will list magazines and periodicals by subject matter covered. You can find the great majority of horticulturally-oriented magazines (both professional and amateur) by looking under the headings of Horticulture or Gardening. There are a few other headings you might check out for certain specialties (such as: Agriculture, Country Living, Ecology, Environmental, Hydroponics, Alternative Lifestyles, Greenhouses, Nurseries, Herbs, Vegetables, etc.).

Once you locate the magazine titles, then see if they are carried by the library. Only large libraries will carry most of the periodicals dealing with special professions. The titles not in the library can possibly be borrowed free by interlibrary loan (check with the loan department at your library). Or the magazine can be contacted directly to purchase a sample copy, or perhaps they will even send a free one if you sound like a serious potential subscriber. Another place you can locate the name and address of most horticulturally-oriented magazines is in the American Horticultural Society's book which is listed below. This book will not, however, have phone numbers and circulation data.

Job listings are usually found in the classified sections of these magazines. Occasionally, the offerings may be fairly numerous.

- **General interest magazines**—There are only a few general interest magazines in the field of horticulture which have classified sections that offer specific positions.

- **Local, state, regional, and national professional or industry organizations**—Check with your county agricultural or horticultural extension agent or with local businesses in the horticultural field; they can advise you if there are professional or industry organizations you might contact for help in gaining employment. For example: almost every state has an association of greenhouse businesses; the same is true for tree growers, perennial growers, garden centers, flower shops, etc. These organizations often have an employment list, or they at least publish job offers in their periodic newsletters. Another way these organizations can be helpful is by providing a list of member businesses to you. This helps you contact individual employers for their job openings.

- **County horticultural or agricultural extension agents**—No matter where you live in the United States, there is an extension agent nearby. Your area may not have a specialist in horticulture but many do.

  Extension agents often serve as unofficial employment brokers since they get around frequently to area businesses that are related to agriculture. Even though your extension agent may not know of any job opportunities, he or she can probably direct you to the local or state professional organizations I mentioned above.

  The county extension office telephone number will be in your phone book. If you can't find it listed under U.S. Government or county extension office (under your county name), ask directory assistance to help you.

  Extension offices are just like any other government office—it may take some explaining to the receptionist to get you in contact with the extension agent most closely associated with horticulture. You don't want the home economist or livestock specialist!

- **Special horticultural reference guides**—There are two special horticultural publications in the United States you should look at for ideas. The most important is:

North American Horticulture Reference Guide
compiled by The American Horticultural Society
7931 East Boulevard Drive
Alexandria, VA 22308
(703) 768-5700

This big book has a lot of information in it, but only a portion is directly useful to job seekers. Borrow it on interlibrary loan if you can because the last copy I purchased was $80.00.

Another smaller publication is titled:

Healthy Harvest—A Global Directory of Sustainable Agriculture and Horticulture Organizations 1992
published by Ag Access
603 Fourth Street
Davis, CA 95616
(916) 756-7177

This book is not nearly so comprehensive but will give you some ideas about employment possibilities and probable contacts.

These two books are not going to point out exactly where you can get a job, but, if you study them carefully, you can easily see how they might be useful. There may be several other references which I am not aware of—keep your eyes open.

- **Internet**—As this communication tool becomes more commonly employed by both information placers and seekers, it will form an important aspect of the total network dealing with horticultural business. There is already a tremendous amount of pertinent information available on the internet, but it is sometimes poorly organized and difficult to find. Searching methods will undoubtedly improve considerably in the near future as will the presentation of data.

  Within a few years, the internet will become so commonly used as to rival traditional information sources such as magazines, books, trade shows, videos, etc. The possibilities are endless and exciting. Anyone who is involved in modern endeavors must quickly adapt to this relatively new phenomenon or risk being left behind in an increasingly sophisticated world. Most of the up-to-date information will soon first appear on the internet—only after a time-lapse will it come out in more traditional forms.

> You must begin now by becoming familiar with useful
> search engines and horticultural web sites. The internet will
> soon bring about a revolution in the way business is conducted.

Now that you have several suggestions about where to look for jobs working with plants, trees, or flowers—get busy!

Decide what type of job you want and start working to generate some employment leads. You will never get anywhere without action.

EVALUATE THE WORK PLACE

Assuming that you have picked a horticultural specialty area to work in and located some prospective employers, there is one final thing you should do before sending your resume or trying to arrange an interview. Check the employer out! See if they are someone you really want to work for.

You can probably learn a good deal about them before you actually go for an interview, at least enough to know whether it is worth your time and theirs to arrange a meeting. After a job interview, you should investigate the employer more thoroughly if you are still interested.

WHAT CHARACTERISTICS DO EMPLOYERS LOOK FOR?

The majority of job seekers mistakenly expect that employers are most interested in the technical ability and previous related job experience of applicants. While this may be so in a limited number of cases, there are many other characteristics which they value as much or more.

Here are some of the important things employers look at (not necessarily arranged in order of importance):

- Honesty.
- Reliability.
- Pleasant disposition.
- Ability to work with others.
- Proficiency in reading, writing, and math skills.
- Ability to organize themselves and others.
- Ability to follow directions accurately and completely.
- Energy.
- Enthusiasm for work.
- Technical knowledge.
- Work experience.
- Flexibility.
- Loyalty to employer.
- Up beat, can do anything attitude.
- Ability to progress and change with circumstances.
- Physical and mental abilities in line with job needs.
- Family life will not unduly interfere with job performance.
- No drug or alcohol abuse.
- Has some interest in doing a good job even when immediate monetary reward is not obvious.
- Reasonable degree of personal hygiene and conduct.
- Previous positive job experience—not necessarily in the present field.

These are all characteristics which you now have or do not have. There is no way you can develop them overnight to prepare for a job interview. But you can do your best to emphasize the ones you have in greatest abundance and play down the ones you do not possess to any extent. Lets face it, no one is perfect—you cannot meet the test in every one of the points mentioned above. Just knowing what characteristics the employer will be looking for will help you prepare for an interview.

HOW TO IMPROVE YOUR CHANCES IN THE JOB MARKET

Here is a list of things you should do (or not do) when applying for employment. As mentioned at the beginning of this chapter, you have seen these suggestions in many other places—but projecting the proper image in an interview is so important that it won't hurt to go over everything again.

- Conduct yourself in a civilized manner.
- Bring a neatly prepared resume.
- Dress properly for the job circumstances.
- Act alive but not nervous.
- Appear confident but not to the point of being a braggart.
- Be prepared but not mechanical.
- Don't get too personal with the employer.
- Do not give false information on any point, even small white lies may come back to haunt you if the employer uncovers them.
- Don't overflow and ramble on, just present the facts and let the employer evaluate them.
- Be precise and keep your responses short.
- Be flexible in any way you can to meet the employer's needs.
- Do not scribble illegibly if you must present any hand written information. Type it out if possible.
- Try to avoid obvious grammatical mistakes in speech—don't use slang or swear words.
- Display a hardworking image.
- Be sure to bring up all your good points—no one else will. But do it as modestly as possible.
- Provide documented evidence of references, abilities, education, awards, special certificates concerning technical proficiency. Have them at your fingertips.
- Provide references as to your honesty.
- Understand completely the terms of any employment situation. Know what the pay is and what is expected of you. Don't be

aggressive in your inquiry but be thorough. The prospective employer will think you are a fool if you don't look out for your own welfare.

- Leave your complete name, phone number, and address. Offer a photograph but don't be offended if the employer doesn't want it; there may be circumstances which make it unlawful for them to accept photographs of job applicants.
- Remember, every situation is unique and may require a slightly different approach to the interview. You can't always follow a cookbook recipe.
- Ask if you should call back—and when.
- Be persistent. If you don't get a particular job the first try, inquire at a later date. This dedication and interest will impress any employer.

THE RESUME

The resume may be viewed as an advertisement which is designed to gain the attention of a potential employer. Often times, the resume will serve as your first significant contact with the employer. As such, it is very important that your resume is designed in such a way that it catches the eye of whomever reads it, thus advancing your application for employment to the top of the heap.

A well-designed resume is an indispensable way with which to "sell yourself."

Conversely, a poorly constructed resume can put you out of the running for a job without the employer giving you a chance. Employers may receive hundreds of resumes when they actively advertise the opening of a position. Reading through this pile of submissions, understandably, can be a mind numbing experience. For your resume to receive the attention it deserves, it must somehow stand out from the crowd.

Although fancy letterhead, multi-colored print, and graphics may grab the eye of the reader, if you go overboard in using them, the resume may be viewed as a product from an adolescent mind. In other words, if you choose to use visual enhancement in constructing your resume, be careful not to over do it— present yourself as a mature professional.

The most important aspect of designing your resume is the packaging of your qualifications so that the employer clearly understands what benefits he or she will gain by hiring you. The qualifications should be listed in order of importance. If you have a college degree but little practical experience, be sure to start out with your education — flaunt your strengths. Again, the major thing you are attempting to convey is **what benefits the employer can gain by hiring you**.

When listing these benefits, be as specific as possible. If you have experience working in a mental hospital, make it known that you are able to communicate with a wide array of people. Be detailed: if you are familiar with farm machinery, list the type, model, make, and any special features of the equipment. Biographical information, such as a clean law record, strong credit history, physical condition, civic activities, etc., can strengthen your resume. Choose only those aspects of your biography which will be viewed positively by the employer. Never volunteer negative information.

Many people employ the use of professional writing services to generate resumes. These services can cost anywhere from $50 to $100. Although these services, more often than not, create professional looking products, the writers do not, and cannot, know your strengths and the specific details about those strengths better than you. If all you are lacking is a computer to create letterhead, graphics, etc., most major copy centers (Kinkos, CopyMax) provide terminals on a rental basis. By designing your own resume, you not only save money, you end up with a superior product.

The following example is provided only to give you a general model of a resume. Each resume, like each individual, is unique. It is your job to manipulate the model so that you achieve the best advertisement of yourself as possible. Remember, you are selling yourself. As in any advertisement, the potential buyer should be made fully aware of what he or she will gain by purchasing the product.

Jane Doe

1 Maple Street ~ Westville, NE 99772
Fax (111) 555-9876 ~ Phone (111) 555-2468 ~ Email jane@server.org

Employment Inquiry/Application

◆ PERSONAL

Describe yourself to the potential employer. State your objective. Include pertinent biographical information. These are the first sentences the reader will view. Attempt to create attention with interesting points and enthusiasm. Be brief. Explain to potential employers precisely why you will be an asset to their organization.

◆ EDUCATION

Degree obtained, school name, year of graduation.
Degree obtained, school name, year of graduation.
Degree obtained, school name, year of graduation.
Pertinent courses.
Special awards, grants, relevant extracurricular activities.

◆ EMPLOYMENT

Dates:
(19** to 20**)   *Position, Name of Company*
Describe your job responsibilities. Use action words to lend impact to the writing. Be **specific**; remove all unnecessary words and phrases. Include the **specific** results of your actions or decisions.

Dates:	*Position, Name of Company* In the same manner as above, describe your next job.
Dates:	*Position, Name of Company* In the same manner as above, describe your next job.
Dates:	*Position, Name of Company* In the same manner as above, describe your current or most recent job.

◆ INTERESTS & ACTIVITIES

List only those interests and activities that you regularly participate in.
Include only those activities employers will view positively.

◆ COMPUTER SKILLS

List software applications, operating systems, and pertinent hardware information.
Include years of experience, or describe your level of knowledge.

◆ LANGUAGES

List the language in which you are most fluent.
List any other languages in which you are fluent.

◆ LET THE EMPLOYER KNOW YOU WILL BE HAPPY TO PROVIDE FURTHER INFORMATION UPON REQUEST.

Chapter 4

HOW TO ADVANCE IN THE JOB YOU FIND

Finding the job is only the first step in launching a successful horticultural career. Your first day at work is none too soon to begin planning on how you intend to keep the job and how you can use it for advancement. Everyone wants to be paid more and move on to a more challenging position—it is simply human nature to become unsatisfied with the status quo. Advancement in employment status will not be automatic; plan ahead to ensure that you make steady forward progress.

HOW TO KEEP A JOB

The characteristics that employers look for which were listed at the end of Chapter 3 should be reviewed after you find employment. They are important not only in landing a job but also in keeping it. If you consistently work at developing these attributes, you will remain employed. There are a few additional points which will make your job more secure.

- Understand the etiquette of employer/employee business relationships and do not cross the line.
- Don't cause problems, your boss has enough already.
- Make an effort to understand your supervisor's methods of operation. Try to get on the same mental "wavelength."
- Do not get in the way or create embarrassing situations by making yourself conspicuous. Let your good work speak for you.
- Always have in mind that your productivity is essential to keeping the company profitable and your job secure.
- Don't be careless with company property or with your own safety or that of other employees.
- Don't expect constant praise for a job you are getting paid to do.
- Diversify your skills to handle other jobs at the workplace— just in case yours is eliminated.

After over 30 years of supervising all types of employees, I am still amazed at the night and day differences which can exist between workers. Some are pleasant and make the work progress smoothly and enjoyably, while others seem to make every day more unproductive and less pleasant than the previous one. No doubt many workers could also say the same for bosses.

Workers and employers must both make a conscious effort to consider the other's welfare—a business or institution cannot operate profitably or successfully without cooperation between the two. Always remember that there is no employment for anyone when the entire project is a failure. Your job as an employee is to contribute towards the overall success of the venture.

JOB ADVANCEMENT

If you have followed the suggestions given up to this point, you will certainly be well on the road toward job advancement. Here are some additional pointers which relate specifically to advancement:

- Try to evaluate advancement potential before you accept employment. Look the workplace over to see if there is room for your progress. Ask questions!
- Show your employer that you are ready to advance by completing every task thoroughly and completely. Try to develop some speed after you become familiar with the work.
- Be realistic about what you can handle: don't try to advance faster than your capabilities.
- In your efforts to advance, show that you are capable of handling other jobs. But don't step on someone else's toes by invading their territory.
- Advancement seldom comes by trying to become buddies with the boss.
- Always try to learn and improve your job skills each day— soon you will become indispensable.
- Advanced positions generally require training in specific technical skills or in the ability to manage people. Try to prepare yourself in these two areas by attending schools, reading professional books, and asking questions.
- In many cases, advancements in pay will depend upon you asking for a raise. If your company does not have a well defined and generally well known pay scale, it may be incumbent upon you to bring up the subject if your supervisor does not do so within a reasonable length of time. This is a delicate area so be sure you handle it tactfully.

  It is best if you find out the general procedures in this area before you go to work. Some companies and institutions will have a definite schedule and guidelines, while others leave the matter up in the air.
- Keep in mind that advancement sometimes depends upon a change of employers. There may not be room for continued upward progress at your first place of employment. Be sure to cultivate good references in your present position; they may be important in landing a job at another company.
- In most cases, there is an upper limit to advancement when you work for someone else. The only practical means of

achieving total career success is by owning your own horticultural business. Information and order blanks for several books about this subject are available inside the back cover.

- Realize that success in this world is sometimes dependent upon lady luck. If you do everything right and advancement doesn't come as soon as expected, just keep pointed in the right direction until your luck changes—it always does if you help it along.

Chapter 5

A SUMMARY OF THINGS TO DO

Now that you have finished quickly reading this material about employment, return to it in a few days and study the contents more carefully. After going through it the second time, you will be ready to start drawing up a detailed plan for seeking employment in the horticultural field.

Follow these guidelines as you plan a course of attack:

- Narrow your choices down to 2 or 3 areas of interest. You can't effectively try to research every imaginable field.
- Keep some alternatives in mind if your first choices don't pan out.
- Gather up whatever information and resources which you may need.
- Be systematic in your research. Don't omit necessary things just because they don't interest you at the time.
- Thoroughly plan your course of action and write it down. Make a check list of essential points.
- Prepare a time schedule for positive action. Make sure your schedule takes into account the peaks of seasonal activity present in many horticultural specialties.

- Execute your plan in a determined manner. Do not let distractions get in the way. Be persistent.
- Take advantage of any special programs which are available. There may be free educational or job training programs that can give you a boost towards employment. Check with your state employment service, as most offer programs which will pay part of your salary for training in a new employment skill. This is a big incentive for companies to hire you.
- Do not force yourself into a choice of fields or specific employment. Just let all the accumulated information simmer in your head—the answer will come eventually without conscious effort.

PART III

FIELD STUDIES IN ORNAMENTAL HORTICULTURE

Chapter 1

PREPARING FOR FIELD STUDIES

There is no better way to gain insights into the ornamental plant industry than to observe how it works on a daily basis. The practical experience gathered while actually visiting horticultural facilities can be used to reinforce and amplify written information. And, in many cases, you will pick up facts and general impressions in the field which were not fully expressible by the written word.

If you wish to work or operate a business in horticulture, carefully planned visits to all sorts of facilities will provide invaluable background information upon which to base future decisions. Field trips broaden knowledge while working on daily problems.

Even serious amateurs who have no commercial interests can benefit from planned visits to horticultural facilities. The following field exercises direct attention toward some specific operational details which the average person is unlikely to notice with a casual visit.

The specific field trips listed below are arranged into groups which display common characteristics and which will require similar observational techniques. By arranging them in this manner, it is possible to reduce the number of individual forms required and thereby make it easier for participants to concentrate upon learning new material. Each general group of field exercises can be completed by using a common form for that group (participants are authorized to make photo copies of these forms for multiple use and should do so before any answers are filled in). This exception to copyright law is granted by Andmar Press only to the original purchaser of *Plants For Profit* and only for the personal use of the buyer. **Do not write in this book if borrowed from the library.**

LIST OF POSSIBLE FIELD EXERCISES

A. Plant production facilities
1. Greenhouse
2. Tree or shrub nursery
3. Sod farm, lawn grass
4. Christmas tree farm
5. Herbaceous perennial farm
6. Cut flower farm

B. Sales facilities
1. Chain store indoor plant sales
2. Chain store outdoor plant sales
3. Independent flower shop
4. Independent garden center
5. Herb store
6. Farmers market
7. Wholesale market, generally cut flowers

C. Landscape and conservation projects
1. Private homes, neighborhoods
2. Estate gardens
3. Businesses, theme parks, etc.
4. City, state, county parks; university, college, major building landscapes
5. Highway installations
6. Mines, dams, industrial reclamation
7. Interior plant displays in malls, convention centers, major buildings

D. Institutional facilities
1. University and college greenhouse gardens
2. Arboretums (tree collections)
3. Botanic gardens
4. Test gardens associated with seed companies, agricultural extension, private & public displays
5. Non-commercial greenhouses
6. Parks department plant growing operations
7. Government plant facilities—Forest Service, Dept. Agriculture, etc.
8. University experiment stations
9. Public gardens

E. Shows, meetings, organizations
1. Master Gardeners organization
2. Local garden club
3. Plant society meetings
4. Horticultural trade shows
5. Garden and horticultural tours

6. State or national horticultural meetings

7. Home and garden shows

F. Library facilities

1. Public library

2. University, college library

3. Agricultural extension library

4. Botanic garden, public garden, arboretum
   libraries

HOW TO PREPARE FOR AND CONDUCT FIELD EXERCISES

Field trips can be an invaluable source of information if they are performed conscientiously. They can be a total waste of time when preparation and careful execution are lacking. Be sure you plan ahead to make your trips successful.

Many of the suggested locations for field exercises will obviously be familiar to you. But there are others which you will need to locate in the phone book or through other sources. Local garden enthusiasts, the Agricultural Extension Agent, garden clubs, owners of horticultural businesses, parks directors, and college horticulture teachers are likely sources where you will also be able to find the locations of facilities for potential field trips.

Not every locality will have a full spectrum of horticulturally related facilities for you to visit. But at least 1/2 of the ones listed should be present in or near every small town.

Look over the prepared field exercise forms carefully before you arrive at a facility. Resolve any questions you might have about the forms before you begin work. Be sure you know how to fill them out properly and that you have a general idea of what information you are looking for. If you are well prepared, you can spend the time available for productive work rather than organizing preliminary details which should have been taken care of previously.

There are some further points to consider when planning a field trip. Most of them are concerned with courtesy to the operators of the facility or with your personal comfort.

- Make sure you realize the difference between public facilities and those which are considered private. Libraries, botanic gardens, garden shows, retail sales areas, etc. are generally open to the public and require no advance notice to visit. Plant production facilities, reclamation sites, private estate gardens, seed company test gardens, etc. usually will require advance contact to make certain an educational visit is allowable. There are some sites which might fall between the two extremes (such as small independent retail shops, parks department facilities, university greenhouses, garden club meetings, etc.).
- If you are in doubt about whether you need permission— ask. It will seldom be denied if you are courteous and explain the purpose of your visit.
- Make sure the operators of private facilities know you are not a nosy inspector or potential competitor.
- If the trip involves outdoor work, dress properly for the weather. Be prepared for mud and cold or dry and hot weather. You may encounter both in the same day.
- Try to visit outdoor facilities during good weather.
- Watch your step—especially in production areas. Numerous hazards may be present.
- Use the rest room before you depart. Some places may have minimal or hard to locate facilities.
- Choose a good time of the year when there is plenty of interesting activity going on. Many horticultural facilities have

very seasonal activity patterns. But don't choose the very busiest days of the year—the owner or manager will often deny access at these times.

- Don't pester the employees or manager. A few questions may be permitted at private facilities but more are a nuisance. In public facilities, it is OK to ask lots of questions—the people are there to help you.
- You should visit facilities of different size and different emphasis. Don't simply choose the biggest and best. There are also things to learn at the less successful facilities.
- Above all, be courteous.
- You are responsible for filling in the field exercise questionnaire sheets as best you can. Do not waste the time of the manager or employees by asking them to help you with questionnaires. You will learn more by making your own evaluations. If you cannot possibly answer some of the questions through your own observations—leave them blank.
- Spend at least 1 hour at each field trip location. In my experience, the average investigator who analyzes the facility carefully will spend at least 2 hours while many observers can find plenty of interesting material for a 4 or 5 hour visit—depending upon the location.
- Andmar Press grants the original purchaser of *Plants For Profit* exception to copyright laws in order to make multiple copies of field exercises. This exception applies only to the personal use of the original owner and specifically does not allow reproduction by any means of additional material in this book.

Chapter 2

FIELD STUDY FORMS

PRODUCTION FACILITY FIELD EXERCISE

Suggested observation outline and questionnaire

1. What is the name of this facility?

2. What type of business or combination business is it?

3. What types of ornamental crops are grown here?

4. Can you name some of the more important species of plants being grown at this site?

5. Would you describe the physical location as urban, suburban, or rural?

6. Can you estimate the total size of this facility in square feet or acres?

7. On the separate grid sheet page provided, draw a rough map of the site layout with all buildings and special features.

8. Does this production facility have a retail sales area on site or at another location, or does it market exclusively through wholesale channels?

9. Do you know what the general market area covered by this firm is?

10. How long has this firm been in business?

11. Make a short list of the major items of machinery and vehicles you notice on site.

12. How many employees have you seen on site?

13. Is there a specific area for employees to have break and clean up?

14. Does the site appear to offer reasonably safe conditions for employees and visitors?

15. Is there a centralized work area or does it seem that most work projects are carried on all over the place?

16. Is the entire business site organized and clean? Somewhat? Disorganized and trashy?

17. Do the crops look healthy and in an appropriate condition so that you would expect consumers to readily purchase them if the price was reasonable?

18. Does this facility appear to mix its own soil or does it purchase bagged soil mix from specialists?

19. Do the outdoor roadways and indoor aisles allow plenty of room for movement of people and crops?

20. Does this facility obtain water from: Wells? Municipal supply? Pond? Stream?

21. Is this the time of year you would expect the production facility to be reasonably busy?

22. How many of this particular type of production facility are listed in your local phone book yellow pages?

23. What is the most important point you learned from this field exercise?

SALES FACILITY FIELD EXERCISE

Suggested observation outline and questionnaire

1. What is the name of this facility?

2. What type of business or combination business is it?

3. What are the main types of horticultural crops sold here?

4. Does the retail facility appear to be a chain store (mass market) type or does it appear to be an independent store operated by an individual, family, or limited number of partners?

5. Is the store located in an urban, suburban, or rural area?

6. On the grid sheet provided, draw a rough map of the facility layout. Be sure to include outdoor sales areas if they are present.

7. Are the displays of plants clean and orderly?

8. Do you feel the horticultural products are displayed properly to accomplish maximum sales?

9. How would you rate the quality of plant material available at this facility? Good, medium, poor?

10. Is there an associated plant production facility on this retail site?

11. Are there plenty of sales people available to help or is this a more or less self service facility?

12. Are there plenty of signs to help customers shop?

13. Is everything clearly priced?

14. Do you feel the varieties of plants offered here for outdoor use are the proper ones for this climatic region?

15. Is there a good choice of plant material?

16. Does it appear that the plant material is being watered and cared for on an appropriate schedule?

17. Have you noticed any plant pests or apparent plant diseases which would cause customers to reject particular plants on sale at this facility?

18. Do the prices for plant material appear to be reasonable considering the quality, selection, and service available at this store?

19. Are there plenty of check out stations for the amount of business being done?

20. Is there plenty of free parking?

21. Is this facility open year-round?

22. Is this the time of year you would expect this facility to be reasonably busy?

23. Does this store offer a publicly stated guarantee policy which you feel is adequate?

24. How long has this store been in operation?

25. How many of this type of facility are doing business in your locality?

26. What is the most important point you have learned from this field exercise?

LANDSCAPE AND CONSERVATION PROJECT FIELD EXERCISE

Suggested observation outline and questionnaire

1. Is this a public (tax supported) or private project?

2. Is the main purpose of this project beautification, or utilitarian (reclamation, playing fields, etc.), or both in combination?

3. Is this project professionally planned and installed or is it done by amateurs?

4. What are the main types of vegetation being utilized for this project (trees, flowers, lawn, etc.).

5. List some of the major plant varieties used in this project.

6. What is the approximate number of square feet or acres included in this project?

7. On the grid sheet page provided, draw a rough map of the project layout. Be sure to distinguish the main physical features and types of vegetation being used.

8. What is the main feature of this project which catches your eye immediately?

9. Are the vegetation and physical features of this project well-maintained?

10. Was this project planned so that it provides beautification on a year around basis rather than for limited times?

11. How long do you estimate this project has been installed?

INSTITUTIONAL FACILITY FIELD EXERCISE

Suggested observation outline and questionnaire

1. What is the name of this facility?

2. What type of institution is this?

3. What is the main purpose of this facility?

4. List the major features of this facility (buildings, grounds, growing areas, work areas, etc.).

5. What are the main species or groups of plants grown or displayed here?

6. Approximately how many square feet or acres is included in this facility?

7. On the grid sheet page provided, draw a rough map of the project layout.

8. Is this facility tax supported or private?

9. Do many people seem to use this facility?

10. Is this the season you would expect people to visit the facility?

11. Does this facility seem to serve a worth while purpose?

12. Are there any major operational problems you can see at this facility?

SHOWS, MEETINGS, ORGANIZATIONS FIELD EXERCISE

Suggested observation outline and questionnaire

1. What is the name of this show, meeting, or organization?

2. What is its main purpose or objective?

3. Who is participating in this show, meeting, or organization (business people, men, women, age, amateurs, homeowners)?

4. Do the participants seem to be heavily involved in horticulture? moderately? slightly?

5. Can you think of any ways this show, meeting, or organization might be of significance to commercial horticulture?

6. How many people are present at this show, meeting, or organization?

7. What are the main impressions or facts you gained from observing this show, meeting, or organization?

LIBRARY FIELD EXERCISE

Suggested observation outline and questionnaire

1. What is the name of this library?

2. Approximately how many books in the horticulture, gardening, agriculture, and botany sections of this library have some relationship to ornamental horticulture? How many magazines?

3. Give the name of at least one reference guide in which you can find all the published periodicals (magazines) listed which pertain to horticulture and gardening (if you cannot find one, ask the librarian to show you how to locate and use such periodical guides).

4. List the most important type of information which is given about magazines in the periodical guide.

5. Can you think of any other subject areas besides horticulture, gardening, agriculture, and botany where you might find information in this library which relates to ornamental horticulture?

6. Write the name of at least 2 periodicals or books useful in commercial horticulture which you have found present in the library. Make sure you have examined the general contents of each one carefully.

7. Do the horticultural titles in this library seem up to date (published recently)?

8. Does this library have an interlibrary loan program with major libraries which are more likely to have a greater amount of material related to ornamental horticulture?

9. Do you think this library has an adequate selection of subject matter about ornamental horticulture?

10. If you cannot find appropriate information in this library, what other local facilities are there where you might locate such material?

INTERNET EXERCISE

The Internet is a revolutionary invention which can potentially make unlimited information available to anyone who has access to a computer equipped with a modem. Although the Internet and the World Wide Web are technically separate entities, for the purposes of this discussion the terms are interchangeable. Discovered by physicists, this computer-based information superhighway can, if employed properly, make the gathering of information necessary for success in business easier and more fruitful than ever before. The Internet is a tool which cannot be ignored. Proper navigation of the World Wide Web can enhance the success of your business. By keeping abreast of the latest trends and information in your field of endeavor, you gain the benefit of valuable knowledge, and, often times, the information is free.

There are, however, a few problems with this seemingly miraculous discovery. The major problem is the issue of findability. Due to the tremendous growth of websites and surfers, the information superhighway is cluttered with cul-de-sacs and false exits. In other words, the Internet, increasingly, can be viewed more as a labyrinth than a clearly marked highway. The people responsible for creating the search engines failed to utilize the time tested-methods of categorization employed by librarians; they ignored library science. This was a critical oversight for which there is no quick cure.

Another problem concerning findability and the search engines is the number of search engines and the (for lack of a better term) esoteric means which each engine uses to retrieve documents. There are hundreds of search engines and each one uses a different method of document retrieval. Because there has never been a uniform classification system put into place before web pages are submitted, the result is a mishmash of information which, more often than not, makes the search for specific material (unless the terminology used in the search is decidedly technical or scientific) tedious and time consuming.

There are also the reverse engineers or "hackers" who manipulate search engines by analyzing document retrieval methods. When these reverse engineers or, to use a literary term, deconstructionists, "hack" a search engine, they are able to utilize the data to promote their (or their employers') web sites and pages to the top of that particular search engine. If you are familiar with web surfing, you undoubtedly have experienced a search which yields illogical results. For example, you search the terms "greenhouse and pesticides," and the top 10 results have nothing to do with either of these terms. This is the way of the World Wide Web. As of yet, there is no clear way to deal with this problem. It would take an army of librarians years to classify the documents which already exist on the web, let alone the thousands upon thousands which are added each day.

Finally, beware of the false informaton which abounds on the World Wide Web. In cyberspace, anyone can be a self-professed expert. Always verify any information taken from the Web.

Still, the World Wide Web can provide a wealth of information if you have the patience to look for it. Carefully choosing the words which will define your search may eliminate a number of false leads. When a search yields poor results, try another combination of words to narrow the field of your search. Navigating the World Wide Web takes cunning and patience. With a little practice, you will soon find that your time is well spent.

Internet Practical

As stated earlier, you can find virtually anything on the World Wide Web. As such, it is important to narrow the search in order to avoid hours of wasted time and eye strain. Since this book is concerned with income opportunities in horticulture, it would prove most useful to begin narrowing the search at this point. Below you are asked to find specific sites concerning horticulture. After successfully completing this lesson, you will be equipped with the necessary skills to help you find all kinds of business information.

On a separate piece of paper, research the topics listed below. Be thorough, the only one you cheat by skimping is yourself.

1. Find the site of your state's Department of Agriculture.

a) Do they offer any services?

b) How can you implement these services into your horticultural enterprise?

c) What kind of information do they provide that could be beneficial (or detrimental) to your proposed operation?

2. Locate the sites of three U.S. Agricultural Extension Offices.

a) How are they the same?

b) How are they different?

3. Find sites providing technical information concerning:

a) Roses.

b) Orchids.

c) Poinsettias.

Did you find conflicting information in the culture of roses? Orchids? Poinsettias?

4. Search for the U.S. Department of Commerce site.

a) Find the Weather Bureau.

b) Analyze weather averages/extremes in your area.

5. Find the Environmental Protection Agency site.

a) Do they offer any services?

b) Do they post regulations which may effect your

business?

6. Locate the site of your state's Department of Environmental Quality or equivalent agency.

a) Do they offer any services?

b) Do they post regulations that may effect your business?

7. Search for the U.S. Small Business Administration site.

a) Can you find any information which may be beneficial to your proposed operation?

b) Are there any programs in which you might want to enroll?

8. Find the U.S. Department of Agricultural Statistics site.

a) Analyze crop production schedules.

9. Locate three greenhouse and/or nursery association sites.

a) Is there a local chapter?

b) Is there a state chapter?

c) What benefits would you gain by joining the association?

10. Search for three horticultural trade show sites.

a) What do the trade shows offer?

b) What would you gain by attending each trade show?

11. Find three greenhouse or nursery magazine sites.

a) Which magazines would you consider subscribing to?

b) Why?

Name of Facility_____

    Grid sheet for recording layout of facilities visited on field trip. Label vertical and horizontal divisions in appropriate scale (multiples of feet).

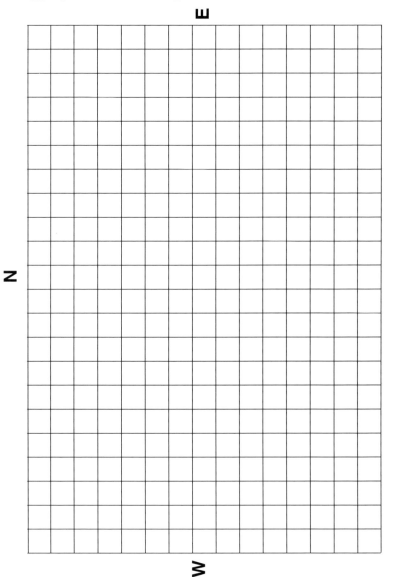

Name of Facility_____

    Grid sheet for recording layout of facilities visited on field trip. Label vertical and horizontal divisions in appropriate scale (multiples of feet).

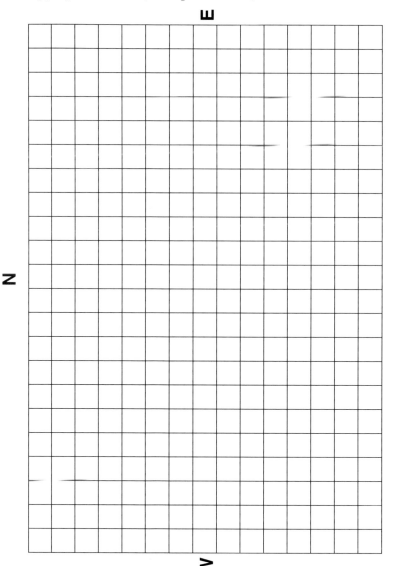

Name of Facility_____

    Grid sheet for recording layout of facilities visited on field trip. Label vertical and horizontal divisions in appropriate scale (multiples of feet).

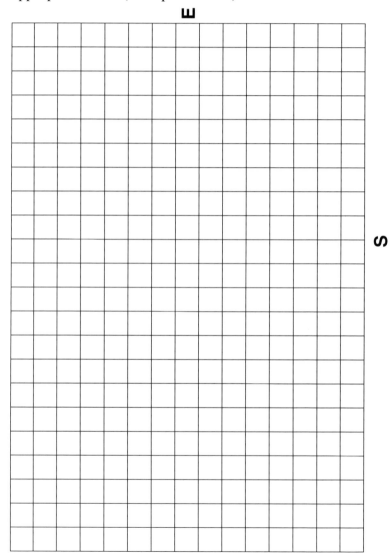

Name of Facility_____

   Grid sheet for recording layout of facilities visited on field trip. Label vertical and horizontal divisions in appropriate scale (multiples of feet).

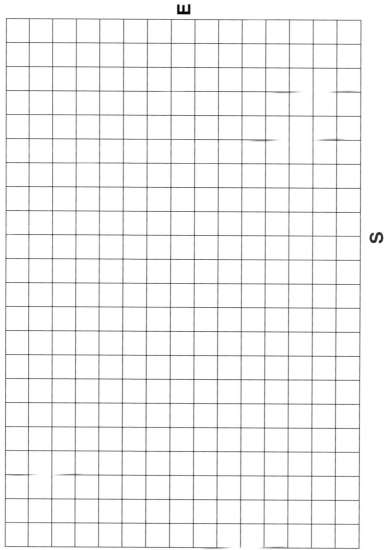

Appendix

USEFUL INFORMATION

Media pH for soilless organic media	
Extremely low	4.5 or less
Slightly low	5.0 to 5.1
Optimum	5.2 to 5.5
Slightly high	5.6 to 5.8
Extremely high	6.9 +

Water quality rating			
Water quality rating	Relative salt content	Reading in micromhos	Reading in ppm
Excellent	low	0-250	167
Good to fair	medium	250-750	167-500
Fair to poor	medium-high	750-2250	500-1500
Poor	excessive	2250+	1500+

Liquid measure

1 level tablespoon	3 level teaspoons
1 cupful	.5 pint 8 fluid ounces 16 tablespoons
1 fluid ounce (U.S.)	29.57 mililiters 2 tablespoons
1 pint (U.S.)	473.2 mililiters 2 cupfuls 16 fluid ounces
1 quart (U.S.)	.9463 liter 2 pints 32 fluid ounces
1 gallon (U.S.)	.1337 cubic foot 231 cubic inches .3785 liter 4 quarts 8 pints 128 fluid ounces

Dry measure

3 level teaspoons	=	1 level tablespoon
16 level tablespoons	=	1 cupful
2 cupfuls	=	1 pint
1 dry pint	=	33.6003 cu. in.
1 dry pint	=	01994 cu. ft.
1 dry pint	=	.55061 liter
2 pints	=	1 quart
1 dry quart	=	67.2006 cu. in.
8 quarts	=	1 peck
4 pecks	=	1 bushel

Ounces to Grams conversion

Ounces	Grams	Ounces	Grams
1/2	14.175	1/256	.111
1	28.349	1/128	.221
2	56.698	1/64	.443
Seed quantities often measured in these sizes >>		1/32	.886
		1/16	1.772
		1/8	3.544
		1/4	7.087

Decimal gallon/ounce equivalents		
.25 gallon	=	32 ounces
	or	1 quart
.5 gallon	=	64 ounces
	or	2 quarts
.75 gallon	=	96 ounces
	or	3 quarts
1.0 gallon	=	128 ounces
	or	4 quarts

Percent to ratio conversions		
2.0%	=	1:50
1.0%	=	1:100
0.8%	=	1:128
0.5%	=	1:200

Loan repayment table	
Term Amount: $10,000	
Interest: 7%	
5 years:	$198.02 per month
10 years:	$116.11 "
15 years:	$89.89 "
20 years:	$77.53 "
25 years:	$70.68 "

Pot volumes	
Pot size	Number filled by 1 cubic yard
4" standard	1,293
4" azalea	1,616
6" standard	397
6" azalea	488.7
8" standard	176

Farenheit/Celsius conversion

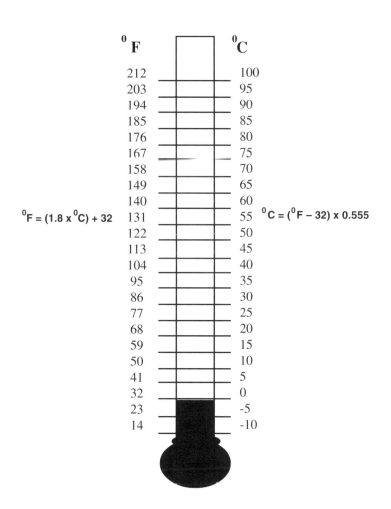

^{0}F

^{0}C

^{0}F	^{0}C
212	100
203	95
194	90
185	85
176	80
167	75
158	70
149	65
140	60
131	55
122	50
113	45
104	40
95	35
86	30
77	25
68	20
59	15
50	10
41	5
32	0
23	-5
14	-10

^{0}F = (1.8 x ^{0}C) + 32

^{0}C = (^{0}F − 32) x 0.555

Metric equivalent

1 square centimeter	=	.1550 square inches
1 square inch	=	6.452 square centimeters
1 square decimeter	=	.1076 square feet
1 square foot	=	9.2903 sq. decimeters
1 square meter	=	1.196 square yards
1 square yard	=	.8361 square meters
1 acre	=	160 square rods
1 square rod	=	.00625 acre

Approx. Metric equivalents

1 decimeter	=	4 inches
1 meter	=	1.1 yards
1 kilometer	=	5/8 mile
1 kilogram	=	2 1/5 pounds
1 metric ton	=	2,204.6 pounds

Metric vs. English measurement

1 centimeter	=	.3937 inch
1 inch	=	2.54 centimeters
1 foot	=	30.48 centimeters
1 meter	=	39.37 inches
1 meter	=	100 centimeters
1 meter	=	1.094 yards
1 meter	=	1,000 millimeters
1 yard	=	.914 meter
1 mile	=	1609.344 meters
1 kilometer	=	1000 meters
1 kilometer	=	.62317 mile
1 sq. centimeter	=	.155 sq. inches
1 cubic centimeter	=	.061 cubic inches
1 fluid ounce	=	29.54 milliliters
1 liter	=	1.057 quarts

LD$_{50}$ – Probable lethal quanities of orally ingested substances related to various human LD 50 ranges

LD$_{50}$: The lethal dosage for 50% of test animals expressed as milligrams of toxicant per kilogram of body weight.

EPA category rating	EPA pesticide label "signal" word
I. Highly Hazardous	Danger–Poison
II. Moderately Hazardous	Warning
III. Slightly Hazardous	Caution
IV. Relatively nonhazardous	Caution

LD 50 range	Quantity of substance ingested orally
I. 0 to 50 mg.	A taste or a few drops.
II. 50 to 500 mg.	1 teaspoon to 2 tablespoons or 1 ounce.
III. 500 to 5000 mg.	2 tablespoons or 1 ounce to 1 pint or pound.
IV. 5000 mg or over.	Over 1 pint or pound.

Lethal Doses of common substances

Aspirin	1750 mg
Caffeine	200
Nicotine	50
Tylenol	3700

U.S. Cooperative Extension Service

Write to the main office in your state for helpful literature, information on soil testing, and specific information concerning your particular crop. Or call the local office if your county has one.

Alabama
Auburn University
Auburn, AL 36849

Alaska
University of Alaska
Fairbanks, AK 99701

Arizona
University of Arizona
Tucson, AZ 85721

Arkansas
P.O. Box 391
Little Rock, AR 72203

California
University of California
2200 University Ave.
Berkeley, CA 94720

Colorado
Colorado State University
Fort Collins, CO 80523

Connecticut
University of Connecticut
Storrs, CT 06269

Delaware
University of Delaware
Newark, DE 19716

District of Columbia
Federal City College
1424 K. Street NW
Washington, D.C. 20005

Florida
University of Florida
Gainesville, FL 32611

U.S. Cooperative Extension Service (cont.)

Georgia
University of Georgia
Athens, GA 30602

Hawaii
University of Hawaii
Honolulu, HI 96822

Idaho
University of Idaho
Morill Hall
Moscow, ID 83843

Illinois
University of Illinois
Urbana, IL 61801

Iowa
Iowa State University
Ames, IA 50011

Kansas
Kansas State University
Manhattan, KS 66506

Kentucky
University of Kentucky
Lexington, KY 40546

Louisiana
Louisiana State University
Baton Rouge, LA 70803

Maine
University of Maine
Orono, ME 04469

Maryland
University of Maryland
College Park, MD 20742

Massachusetts
University of Mass.
Amherst, MA 48824

Michigan
Michigan State University
East Lansing, MI 48824

Minnesota
University of Minnesota
St. Paul, MN 55455

Mississippi
Mississippi State Univ.
Mississippi State, MS
39762

U.S. Cooperative Extension Service (cont.)

Missouri
University of Missouri
Columbia, MO 65211

Montana
Montana State University
Bozeman, MT 59717

Nebraska
University of Nebraska
Lincoln, NE 68588

Nevada
University of Nevada
Reno, NV 89557

New Hampshire
Univ. of New Hampshire
Taylor Hall
Durham, NH 03824

New Jersey
Rutgers — The State Univ.
New Brunswick, NJ 08903

New Mexico
New Mexico State Univ.
Las Cruces, NM 88003

New York
New York State Col. of Ag.
Ithaca, NY 14853

North Carolina
North Carolina State Univ.
Raleigh, NC 27695

North Dakota
North Dakota State Univ.
Fargo, ND 58105

Ohio
Ohio State University
Columbus, OH 43210

Oklahoma
Oklahoma State Univ.
Stillwater, OK 74078

Oregon
Oregon State University
Corvallis, OR 97331

Pennsylvania
Pennsylvania State Univ.
University Park, PA 16802

U.S. Cooperative Extension Service (cont.)

Puerto Rico
University of Puerto Rico
Rio Piedras, Puerto Rico
00931

Rhode Island
University of Rhode Island
Kingston, RI 02881

South Carolina
Clemson University
Clemson, SC 29634

South Dakota
South Dakota State Univ.
Brookings, SD 57007

Tennessee
University of Tennessee
P.O. Box 1071
Knoxville, TN 37996

Texas
Texas A&M University
College Station, TX 77843

Utah
Utah State University
Logan, UT 84322

Vermont
University of Vermont
Burlington, VT 05405

Virginia
Virginia Polytechnic
Institute and State Univ.
Blacksburg, VA 24601

Washington
Washington State Univ.
Pullman, WA 99164

West Virginia
West Virginia University
Morgantown, WV 26506

Wisconsin
University of Wisconsin
Madison, WI 53706

Wyoming
University of Wyoming
Box 3354, Univ. Station
Laramie, WY 82071

Internet addresses

**United States
Department of Agriculture
Cooperative State Research and Extension Service**
http://www.reeusda.gov/new/csrees.htm

**United States
Department of Agriculture**
http://www.usda.gov

**United States
Agriculture Statistics**
http://www.usda.gov/nass/

**United States
Department of Agriculture
Plants Database**
http://www.plants.usda.gov/plants/plntmenu.html

U.S. Small Business Administration
http://www.sbaonline.sba.gov

**United States
Department of Commerce**
http://www.doc.gov

National Weather Service
http://www.nws.noaa.gov

Internet addresses (cont.)

Plant Web
http://www.plantweb.com
(an excellent source for
horticultural links)

American Horticultural Society
http://www.ahs.org/

American Society of Horticultural Science
http://www.ashs.org/

**American Nursery and Landscape
Association**
http://www.anla.org

Associated Landscape Contractors of America
http://www.alca.org

Southern Nursery Association
http://www.sna.org

National Gardening Association
http://www.garden.org/nga/

LITERATURE

American Nurseryman
American Nurseryman Pub. Co.
77 West Washington St. #2100
Chicago, IL 60602
(312)782-5505
1-800-621-5727

American Vegetable Grower
Meister Publishing Co.
37733 Euclid Ave.
Willoughby, OH 44094
(216) 942-2000
1-800-572-774

Floral Mass Marketing
205 Wacker Dr.
Ste. 1040
Chicago, IL 60606
(312) 739-5000

Florist's Review
(312) 782-5505
1-800-621-5727

Flowers
11444 Olympic Blvd.
4th Floor
Los Angeles, CA 90064
(310) 231-9199

Flower News
205 Wacker Dr. Ste. 1040
Chicago, IL 60606
(312) 739-5000

Garden Supply Retailer
One Chilton Way
Radnor, PA 19089
(610) 964-4269

Greenhouse Business
1951 Rohlwing Rd. Ste. B
Rolling Meadows, IL 60008
(847) 870-1576

Greenhouse Grower
Meister Publishing Co.
37733 Euclid Ave.
Willoughby, OH 44094
(216) 942-2000
1-800-572-7740

Greenhouse Product News
Scranton Gillette Comm., Inc.
380 E. Northwest Hwy.
Ste. 200
Des Plaines, IL 60016
(847) 298-6622

Grower Talks
P.O. Box 9
Batavia, IL 60510
(888) 201-1962

Growers Press, Inc.
P.O. Box 189
Princeton, B.C. Canada
VOX 1WO
1(250) 295-7755

Herbs for Health, Also Herb Companion. And other Herb books
Interweave Press
201 E. 4th St.
Loveland, CO 80537
(970) 669-7672
1-800-645-3675

Interior Landscape
American Nurseryman Publ. Co.
77 W. Washington St., Ste. 2100
Chicago, IL 60602
(312) 782-5505
1-800-621-5727

Nursery Retailer
Brantwood Publications
2410 Northside Dr.
Clearwater, FL 33761
(727) 796-3877

The Growing Edge
P.O. Box 1027
Corvallis, OR 97339
(541) 757-2511

The Herb Quarterly
P.O. Box 689
San Anselmo, CA 94979
1-800-371-HERB

The Soilless Grower
Hydroponic Society of America
P.O. Box 1183
El Cerito, CA 94530
(510) 743-9605

All the following are publications of :

Branch-Smith Publishing
120 St. Louis Ave.
Fort Worth, TX 76104
(817) 332-8236 or 1-800-433-5612

Garden Center Products & Supplies
Garden Center Merchandising & Management
Greenhouse Management & Production
Nursery Management & Production
SAF Magazine

Horticulture- Magazine of American Gardening
98 N. Washington St.
Boston, MA 02114-1913
(617) 742-5600

Fine Gardening
63 S. Main St.
P.O. Box 5506
Newtown, CT 06470-5506
(203) 426-8171

The American Gardener
American Horticultural Society
7931 E. Boulevard Drive
Alexandria, VA 22308-1300
(703) 768-5700

National Gardening
Magazine of The National Gardening Assoc.
180 Flynn Ave.
Burlington, VT 05401
1-800-538-7476

Entrepreneur Magazine
2392 Morse Ave.
Irvine, CA 92614
(949) 261-2325

**Home Business
Magazine**
9582 Hamilton Ave.
Suite 368
Huntington Beach, CA 92646
(714) 968-0331

**American Horticultural
Therapy Association**
9220 Wightman Rd.
Suite 300
Gaithersburg, MD 20879
(303) 331-3862

People Plant Connection
(303) 820-3151

Journal of Theraputic Horticulture
(303) 820-3151

INDEX

BOOKS BY ANDMAR PRESS

Andmar Press offers the following books by Dr. Jozwik about opportunities and methods in commercial horticulture. Mail order delivery to your door is available. Each purchase is fully guaranteed. Cash refunds are honored for any reason if the original invoice is presented.

The Greenhouse and Nursery Handbook
A Complete Guide to Growing and Selling Ornamental Container Plants.
Everything you need to know about how to grow and sell ornamental plants is clearly presented in this large, illustrated volume. The culture of hundreds of bedding plants, flowering pot plants, foliage plants, trees, shrubs, and perennials is covered from A to Z. Basic environmental factors like fertilizers, moisture, temperature, insects, diseases, and soil are explained in terms everyone can understand. *The Greenhouse and Nursery Handbook* is an absolute must for every horticulturist whether their interests are commercial or recreational. Hardcover $97.00 plus $7.00 shipping. 806 pages.

Perennial Plants for Profit or Pleasure
How to Grow Perennial Flowers and Herbs for Profit or Personal Landscape Use.
This book details the exact methods necessary to set up a low cost business growing perennial plants—literally in your own backyard. Or you can use the system to provide economical perennials for parks,

cemeteries, businesses, garden clubs, churches, or home gardens. Every step of production and marketing is clearly pointed out. Convenient sources for supplies are included free. $39.95 plus $5.00 shipping. Hardcover. 300 pages.

How to Make Money Growing Plants, Trees, and Flowers.
A Guide to Profitable Earth-Friendly Ventures.
Outlines the many business opportunities available in horticulture and offers the reader important preliminary information about how to choose a field of interest and how to get started correctly. This book is essential for anyone who needs a concise summary of practical start up advice. $39.95 plus $5.00 shipping. Hardcover. 308 pages.

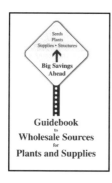

Guidebook to Wholesale Sources for Plants and Supplies
Tells you how to easily obtain beautiful catalogs from leading wholesale horticultural firms. Complete addresses and telephone numbers included to save you time. The companies listed offer a large selection of wholesale supplies and plants which are available only to established professional growers or persons who wish to begin a horticultural business soon. $9.95 plus $3.00 shipping.

Plants for Profit—Income Opportunities in Horticulture

A multifaceted book which presents general information about how to start a horticultural business and then examines details of some specific business and employment opportunities. On site field trip forms are included to familiarize you with the industry. Numerous trade publications are cited for further information. $39.95 plus $5.00 shipping. Hardcover. 304 pages.

NEW!

Illustrated
Guide to
Landscape
Plants

The Illustrated Handbook of Landscape Plants—Includes Trees, Shrubs, Annuals and Perennials.

An indispensable guide to hundreds of North American ornamental species. Illustrated profusely in color to help both professionals and amateurs plan beautiful and ecologically sound landscapes. Details of size, color, and cultural preferences outlined for each variety. Durable 8½ x 11 hardcover notebook style allows professionals to add their own material and drawings for a full open presentation to customers. $29.95 plus $5.00 shipping. New!

Visit Our Website:
http://www.andmar.com

302

ORDER BLANK FOR BOOKS

Please send the following books to me. I understand the total order amount below must be transferred to the reverse side of this page where I will indicate my shipping instructions and deduct any allowable postage discount for orders of more than one title.

Quan.	Title	Price	Shipping	Total
_____	The Greenhouse and Nursery Handbook **Hardback Deluxe Edition**	$97.00	$7.00	$ _____
_____	Perennial Plants for Profit or Pleasure **Hardcover**	$39.95	$5.00	$ _____
_____	Make Money Growing Plants, Trees, and Flowers **Hardcover**	$39.95	$5.00	$ _____
_____	Guidebook to Wholesale Sources for Plants and Supplies	$9.95	$3.00	$ _____
_____	Plants for Profit – Income Opportunities in Horticulture **Hardcover**	$39.95	$5.00	$ _____
_____	The Illustrated Handbook of Landscape Plants **Hardcover**	$29.95	$5.00	$ _____

Total amount due for titles ordered .... $ _____

Canadian and foreign orders must be paid by VISA or MasterCard or by money orders denominated in U.S. dollars. Canadian and U.K. orders add $5.00 additional shipping per order. All other foreign orders add $15.00 additional per order for insured air mail.Orders shipped priority mail where possible.

Please transfer the total order amount to the reverse side of this page and complete all shipping instructions carefully. Enclose full payment by check, credit card, or money order.

FULL MONEY BACK GUARANTEE

SHIPPING AND PAYMENT FORM

Total book order from reverse side of this page .... $ _____

United States and territories customers subtract a
$2.00 postage discount for each title ordered
after the first book .... $ (_____)

Total amount due in U.S. dollars after postage
discount subtracted .... $ _____

Check type of payment enclosed

☐ Visa or MC ☐ Money Order

☐ Check (drawn on U.S. Branch)

Andmar Press

West Yellowstone Highway
P.O. Box 217
Mills, WY 82644-0217

Please Print or Type Clearly

Name_____

Company_____

Address _____

_____

City _____

State/Zip _____

Phone (_____) _____

VISA or MC
Full Number _____

Expiration Date_____

FULL MONEY BACK GUARANTEE

**Please review your order on the reverse side of this page to
make sure both the titles and order total are correct.**